TALES FROM OUR CORNISH ISLAND

Everybody dreams of escaping from it all to a
peaceful, private island of their own. But for
most people escape remains just that, a
dream, a fantasy. Evelyn Atkins and her
sister, Babs, dreamed like everybody else,
but they chased their dream and on
13th February 1965 they spent their first night
on St George's Island off Looe in Cornwall.

Evelyn Atkins told the story of how they
became the owners of the island in WE
BOUGHT AN ISLAND. In this sequel she
describes the adventures and excitements,
hazards and challenges of everyday life on a
remote island.

As the author says, once 'you have been
touched by "island fever" you have been
inoculated for life against the hazards which
will surely beset you' and this book is a
testament to her continuing delight in her
island home.

Praise for WE BOUGHT AN ISLAND

'A delightful story of what happened when the Misses Atkins did what everyone dreams of doing'

Daily Mail

'It takes pluck, optimism and a sense of humour to leave a pleasant house and a circle of friends in suburban Surrey and decamp to an unpeopled island off the coast of Cornwall. Fortunately this sturdy pair had plenty of the right qualities. Here is their engaging account of how they turned dream into reality'

Sunday Telegraph

'Against formidable odds, physically and financially, the dream was realised and this interesting and easily-read book unfolds the tale'

Yorkshire Post

'The age of chivalry is dead, but the time of adventure is not yet past. Miss Atkins' writing is lively, but never lush, plain but never humdrum'

Daily Telegraph

**Also by the same author,
and available from Coronet:**

We Bought An Island

About the Author
Evelyn Atkins, as well as working for many
years for ICI, was actively involved in
mountaineering, various sports, including
small-bore shooting (she is a mastershot and
has represented Surrey at Bisley),
photography and music. During the war she
was an officer with the WRNS. Her time is now
taken up by pottery but, with her sister, Babs
– who retired in 1977 from her position as
Senior Mistress at Looe Secondary School –
she also shares an interest in woodcarving,
gardening, cooking, beekeeping and making
(and drinking) wine.

ST GEORGE'S ISLAND

KEY
1. Generator
2. Smugglers' Cottage
3. Orchard and beehive
4. Daffodil fields
5. Island House
6. Jetty Cottage
7. Flagstaff
8. Bridge
9. Daffodil fields

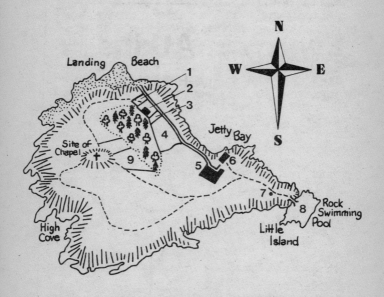

Tales from our Cornish Island

Evelyn E. Atkins

Author of WE BOUGHT AN ISLAND

CORONET BOOKS
Hodder and Stoughton

For Babs

Copyright © Evelyn E. Atkins 1986

First published in Great Britain in 1986
by Harrap Limited
Coronet edition 1987

British Library C.I.P.

Atkins, Evelyn E.
 Tales from our Cornish island.
 1. Looe Island (Cornwall)
 I. Title
 942.3'74   DA670.L/

 ISBN 0 340 40887 1

Printed and bound in Great Britain for
Hodder and Stoughton Paperbacks, a
division of Hodder and Stoughton Ltd.,
Mill Road, Dunton Green, Sevenoaks,
Kent (Editorial Office: 47 Bedford
Square, London, WC1B 3DP) by
Cox & Wyman Ltd., Reading.

CONTENTS

The
PROLOGUE

'What is it like living on an island?' 'How can you possibly live alone there in the winter?' 'Whatever do you do with yourselves?' 'How do you manage for food, water, electricity and so on?' These and similar questions are shot at us *ad infinitum* by the many holiday-makers who visit us during the summer months, incredulous that two sisters, now both retired, should be able to resolve these problems and yet remain, as one gentleman gallantly put it, 'normal'.

This book attempts to answer these questions, although it must be left to the reader to decide if in fact we are 'normal', that is, assuming that normality can be defined. This book also sets out to give an account of our early pioneering days. How we came to acquire an island in the first place, as we were the wrong age, the wrong sex and in the wrong income bracket to make this seem possible, is described in *We Bought An Island*. To the many kind readers from all parts of the world, island lovers all, who have written asking for a sequel, this, in a way, is it. I say 'in a way' for a sequel suggests to my mind, not a resumption, but the end of a story, and these tales, by their very nature, are part of a continuing saga. Even as this is being written incidents crowd in thick and fast. Events are as unpredictable as the weather. The warp and weft of every-day life may have a certain pattern, varying with the seasons, but the adventures and excitements, the hazards and challenges and the ideas that are sparked off add a tumult of colour that bedazzles the onlooker and participant alike. An ordinary action such as the turning on of an electric light switch is fraught with anxiety. Will the generator start up and so give us light? Again when we retire at night will it be stilled as it should by the flick of a light switch in the bedroom? If the pilot light still glows, then, even if a gale is blowing, one must don oilskins to trudge nearly a quarter of a mile down the path to the generator to investigate.

If, on the mainland, you take a walk down the garden path to the road, would you expect to see anything out of the ordinary, except that perhaps the roses have blown down in the wind, the Joneses are painting their house again, or the workmen are digging up the road. A routine walk here down the path that ends on the beach is a daily adventure. What will be found there: a shipwrecked boat? a dead dolphin? a new model boat in full sail? a perfect china owl bobbing in over the rocks in a westerly gale? antique cannon balls? drums of lethal chemicals liable to explode at a touch? a sheep's carcase? furniture in good shape? semi-precious stones? tragically, a dead body? All these and many more have been found at the end of a saunter down *our* path.

Ordinary day-to-day life is highlighted dramatically. Add to this the projects undertaken that the island inspires, and life becomes crowded, leisure an elusive dream.

The difficulty then in satisfying the curiosity of those who would know how we make out on our island is finding the breathing space to sit down and write about it. Life is very much 'now', with our sights set only on the near future. Inevitably there will be unfinished tales and unresolved problems, as indeed there were in the first book not, as one reviewer thought, to whet the appetite of the reader, but because, unlike fiction, where plots must be neatly rounded off, this is about real life, and real life is not parcelled off into self-contained episodes.

Here on the island it is in fact a cross between running a ship and a farm, without crew or farm workers. It seemed an insuperable task to write the first book during the twelve winters or so when I was alone on the island. The writing of this sequel has been eased considerably since my sister, Babs, retired and now lives here all the time. Without her unfailing encouragement it would not have been written at all. She has spurred me on when my spirits flagged and has given unstintingly of her precious time and energy to help and advise me. I am indebted also to the regular voluntary helpers who, during the summer months, have relieved me of some of my share of the day-to-day work of the island. They have backed up Babs — who has been at the helm during the busy summertime — in every possible way. We are both of us grateful to our floating community of friends for their hard work and their versatility.

We have been told that it is refreshing to read a book in which there is no sex or violence. This is not strictly true. There is sex in abundance but it is that of the proliferating wild life, and violence we have in plenty but it is that of the raging seas that pound upon our shores and the storms of up to hurricane force that beat about our heads.

It is impossible to relate all the events and exciting happenings of the past twenty years in one book. This one therefore has been written in the form of tales, each dealing with a different aspect of island life and showing how it has evolved over the years. There are many more such tales to be told and others related here to be continued, for life is changing all the time.

Do you have to be a particular type of person to take to, or more to the point, endure island life? All we can say is that when we first came here we were considered to be the most unlikely would-be islanders and there were some who thought that we should only stick it out for three months. That we have just celebrated our twentieth anniversary here in a raging storm in February 1985 proves that if you have been touched by 'island fever' it matters not at all, for you have been inoculated for life against the hazards which will surely beset you, or so we ourselves hope, as each day dawns.

The
PIONEERS'
Tale

The metallic sound of clip-clopping awakened me from a deep sleep. Bewildered, I sat up surprised to see that, apart from shoes, I was fully dressed. More surprising still I was not in bed but flat on the floor, and I was not alone. The dying embers of a driftwood fire stared at me from a huge stone fireplace, the glow drained of colour by the sunlight streaming through the windows.

Where was I? Who was with me? Why was I sleeping fully clothed on the floor boards of an empty room?

With an exciting thud of my heart memory came flooding back. My sister, Babs, and I had spent the first night on our very own island. How had this come about?

Babs and I had dreamed the impossible dream of owning an island, and by an incredible series of unforeseen events it had come about. For me it was fortuitous that I had retired early so was still active enough to take on what, to all our friends, seemed a daunting challenge. The island, St George's, locally known as Looe island, although only one mile off the south Cornish coast, is pounded by wild seas for many parts of the year so at those times one might as well be 100 miles out in the Atlantic. Although not a desert island — it possesses three dwellings, Island House, two cottages, a generator and many outhouses — it has no inhabitants other than the owners, now miraculously our two selves. Babs, eight years younger than myself, had resigned from a plum job as Deputy Head and Headmistress of a large school in Surrey so that we could come to live here. Luck played a part in that the post of Senior Mistress at Looe County Secondary School became vacant and Babs obtained the appointment. Even so it meant a drop of

several hundreds of pounds a year in her salary. Income-wise I
only had my pension from ICI at whose Head Office I had
worked in London, but we reckoned that the chance of
acquiring our very own island was worth any financial sacrifice,
any risks. Indeed when we burned our boats for this
once-in-a-lifetime opportunity, Babs had resigned her post
with no other job in view, and through early retirement my
pension was quite modest.

No wonder our friends thought that not only were we
foolhardy but stark staring ravers, to roar off westward in
mid-winter to live on an uninhabited island off the wild Cornish
coast with only the certainty of my pension to sustain us. Dame
Fortune, however, decided that we needed some encouragement
for, by the wave of her wand, this senior teaching post became
vacant and magically it became Babs's.

We had previously, following my retirement, bought two
tiny fisherman's cottages in West Looe, one of which was to be a
pottery, my designated second career. With the acquisition of
the island we decided to move the venue of the pottery there,
retain the two cottages — one for holiday lettings to help
subsidize the upkeep of the island, the other for Babs to have as a
pied-à-terre.

The latter was essential, for it soon became apparent that any
commuting between the island and school would be out of the
question. The weather and tides dictate the times when ferrying
is possible. Winter storms and gales in autumn and spring can
cut one off from the mainland for days or even weeks at a time.
Since moving down to Cornwall at Christmas 1964, we had
made several perilous journeys to get our furniture over. This
had been possible only because of the seamanship and daring of
Wren Toms, a young local Cornishman, who had cheerfully and
eagerly taken on the job of transporting us over in the *Orlando*, a
thirty-foot open boat whose only protection from the elements
was a wheelhouse. Nevertheless five journeys in January and
February 1965, had brought all our belongings over, including
a massive eight feet high bookcase, thousands of books and forty
gallons of home-made wine. The consensus of opinion locally

was that we would last three months if we were not drowned
before then.

Wren Toms had a reputation locally of being a daredevil who
took risks, but it appeared to us that he met problems as
challenges to tax his skill, which rightly, he did not
underestimate. The fact is that it was entirely due to his ability
that here we were, in mid-February in raging seas, at last
resident on our island. He had brought us and the last of our
possessions the previous day in fierce north-west squalls.
Conditions were so bad that, once we had landed, he had
advised us to return to the mainland and to come back another
time to stay. We could not see the logic of this and, frustrated as
we were by the abortive attempts to move since Christmas, this
we flatly refused to do. Here we were on our island and here we
meant to stay. There was the small matter that Babs would have
to go back the next day anyway as she was due in school on
Monday; but this Saturday, 13 February 1965, we decided,
history was to be made. It was compulsion to us that that night
our heads should rest on the island. The other heads, being
Toby our faithful, smooth-haired, curly tailed fox-terrier-brand
friend, and Ruth, a girl who was going to help for a few months.

Many had wanted to join us in our project, the main
contenders being Cecily, our niece, her husband Doug and their
family of three children. It was obvious that our own modest
income, without any family allowances or tax relief, would not
run to supporting another family. Therefore any family who
joined us would have to work the land sufficiently to earn the
extra income necessary for their maintenance. We very much
doubted the feasibility of this.

It seemed to us that we needed breathing-space. We would
settle in, we decided, and view the possibilities from first-hand
experience. In any case in those first early days our only desire
was to live on the island, cope with the daffodils, cultivate the
land and, in our leisure time, practise our crafts. We certainly
did not want to take on any extra financial obligations, and we
had no far-reaching plans. For the moment we were content to

enjoy the heady delights of savouring island life. We were still in dreamland and did not want to come down to earth just yet.

When, therefore, Ruth, recently returned home from a stay in the US, her imagination caught by the chance of living on an island, offered to come and help us just for her keep and Insurance Stamp for a few months, we were delighted. No commitments for the future, no financial strain of supporting a family; as a short-term plan it seemed ideal. She could stay until May, when her parents would need her help on their smallholding in Shutta, by Looe. The arrangement had the added bonus that Ruth would have first-hand knowledge of market-gardening. With the island's early spring and the daffodils about to blaze into colour we could do with, if not a man, at least a lady of the soil. Wren, who had a full-time job working for the Council, had offered to help at weekends, as had two schoolboy volunteers. This, then, was our labour force.

This was how it came about that Ruth was the fourth member sleeping on the bare boards of Island House on that wild February Saturday night. It was also the reason for the metallic clip-clopping that had awakened me on the Sunday morning after our first exciting night on the island, for, on investigation, we found that the mysterious sounds that we had heard above the roar of the sea and the haunting cries of the seagulls, were caused by Wren who had left so reluctantly the previous afternoon. He had in fact returned soon after dawn and was chipping a channel through the rocks to the jetty with a pickaxe. It seemed an extraordinary occupation for dawn on a Sunday morning in winter, but Wren was no ordinary person. He loved the island and, as we now realized, because of this, identified himself with our problems and helped us so willingly with our projects.

To those who enjoy the amenities of urban or suburban life the prospect before us would have seemed incredibly primitive. We had come from Epsom Downs on the outer fringes of the Green Belt, with one foot in the country. We had enjoyed a comfortable life in a detached property, all electric, and full of labour-saving devices. To help us also in our full-time busy lives we had a daily help and a weekly gardener. Now we could only have electricity if we could get the generator going ourselves. A six months' period of non-habitation of the island had cancelled out its supposed automatic abilities. This entailed a quarter-mile trek down a muddy track to the generator to swing an enormous handle to get it started. Last thing at night we had to tramp down again to stop it so that the lights would go out, returning and going to bed by the light of an oil lantern.

Our freshwater storage tank had a weed growing in it. Consequently when we turned on the tap in the kitchen for a nice 'cuppa', out gushed a foaming brown liquid with a smell so putrid it had one retching on the spot. The Aga, the only visible form of cooker, was rusted from lack of use and the damp sea-air. An atmosphere of slow decay and death pervaded the whole house with the gloom that descends like a mantle on an old building that has had no human life breathed in it for many moons. In addition to this was the inescapable fact that the only food we had was what we had brought with us, and with the raging seas between us and the mainland, shopping trips seemed remote, to say the least.

This then was the situation that faced us on that first morning on our island of dreams. In retrospect I am sure that most normal people, housewives certainly, would have felt like jumping off the nearest cliff in despair. As only island lovers the world over and through the ages would understand, we did not appreciate the paucity of our situation, for unbelievably it seemed to us that we had attained paradise. Heady with island fever, we saw everything bathed in a rosy glow of achievement. Babs and I looked at each other across the bare boards, the inert and rusting machinery, our toppling piles of furniture strewn like wreckage in the general air of dankness, with unspoken exultation beaming between us. We were on our island at last. Nothing else mattered.

Presently Wren came in from pickaxing the rocks. He had recovered from his disappointment of the day before now that he was in on our adventure again, and was as chirpy as his name.

Emotional like all Celts, he admitted to sinking into a slough of gloom on his return to the mainland the previous day. Now that he was back on the island he was full of enthusiasm again and, over coffee brewed from rain-water over the driftwood fire, he expounded in detail schemes for making a harbour. 'Mind you, it would cost many thousands, and there would be the problem of labour,' he added casually, but immediately brushed aside these two major obstacles and went into great technical details of how it could be achieved. We listened bemused. What a way of spending one's retirement! Builders of harbours indeed! Nevertheless, in our exalted mood, anything seemed possible. Encouraged by our interest and with his contagious enthusiasm and confidence-inspiring manner he took me down to the rocks and showed me how to wield the pickaxe so that I could go on enlarging the channel he was making to the jetty and so, presumably, start the foundations of the harbour. As the resident sister I, apparently, was the one most likely to benefit from his expert tuition and put it into practice.

Of all the activities I had hoped to indulge in in my retirement I had never envisaged pickaxing rocks. However, always willing to learn a new skill, I had a go. I found to my surprise and delight that the cunning use of rhythm, based on early training in eurythmics, gave a certain amount of ease in wielding this fearsome implement, without exerting too much energy, and I was able to chip away to Wren's approval. Nevertheless it was not one of my ambitions to become a lady champion pickaxer. Privately I earmarked this activity for delegation to some future 'friend' more naturally endowed physically than myself. I intended to 'channel' my energies in other directions. Although at the time of writing we have not so far built a harbour, a series of muscular young men, and older ones too, have chipped away and we now have a sizeable channel and, with the tide in, quite big boats can moor up by the jetty.

After Wren had inspected the generator and declared that the lack of automation was beyond his skill and knowledge, and a job for the Lister engineer, he prepared to return to the mainland to bring his wife over for a picnic lunch. That the sea was lopping all over the place worried him not in the least. He rowed out to the *Orlando*, went ashore in that and around midday returned with Valerie and a picnic. We thought it very brave and loyal of her to come, for charging across the wild seas in mid-winter for a picnic on an island was not exactly an ideal way of spending a Sunday afternoon. She was dressed rather nicely with a fur tippet to keep out the cold — she also wore high-heeled shoes. Suddenly we felt rather sordid in our jeans which we had slept in all night, and our seaweed encrusted gumboots made us feel like something that the sea had washed up. Valerie produced a delectable picnic lunch and we fell on her delicious salmon sandwiches with fervour. We sat on cushions on the floor but managed to find an odd chair for our visitor from the furniture which was amassed higgledy-piggledy in the hall and kitchen. For the first, but not for the last, time since living on the island we felt that we had lost any hostess image that we may have had in our previous existence.

After coffee, to the accompaniment of more big talk of future plans, mostly about harbours and the like, we came down to earth to the more mundane task of settling in. Valerie helped move some of our books down to the dwelling above the jetty — this we later named Jetty Cottage. From here we could see a door built into the cliffs above the jetty beach. To reach it one had to climb up some stone steps built on to the rocks below. This, incredibly, was the entrance to the source of our freshwater supply. We subsequently discovered that the island is abundant in fresh water; the difficulty is the vast expense involved in locating its best source, channelling it and storing it against the times of summer droughts. This problem was to dominate our lives and still does. That it has always been a problem was obvious from the signs on the island of several disused and presumably dried up wells. As people of wealth had owned the island in the past it was apparent that it was not an easy problem to solve. The system we had inherited was novel to say the least. The door led to a tunnel which has been bored some thirty or forty feet into the cliff; this acted as a channel for the spring water which flowed into a well which had been

excavated eight feet or so below the entrance. A petrol pump
had been installed on a concrete platform above the well; the
water was pumped up to storage tanks in the woods high above
the daffodil fields, and gravity fed to the three dwellings,
where, in theory, one turned on a tap and out gushed spring
water. Our first job then was to drain the tanks of the putrid
water, sterilize them with the sodium chlorate we had brought
with us and flush them out. We scarcely had time to start on
what was later to prove a mammoth task and to note in passing
that the first daffodils were peeping through, when it was time
for the shore party to embark. Sadly we saw Babs, Wren and
Valerie off. They rowed over the bucking seas to the *Orlando* and
we waved to them as they disappeared into the darkness.

Warmed if not cheered by baked beans and eggs cooked over
the roaring driftwood fire, we filled our flasks with hot
rain-water for a late night drink and coffee in the morning. We
then made our pilgrimage down to the generator to turn it off,
and so up the track again, the lamplight flickering eerily in the
overhanging trees.

Unbeknown to us we were watched by a pair of eyes.

Back in the autumn, the Whitehouses, from whom we had
bought the island, wrote to us in Surrey, from Looe, where they
had already moved so that Mr Whitehouse could have the
medical attention he needed, to ask if we could take up
residence straight away as a cat had refused to leave the island
with them. Their daughter Toni had been rowing over each
week to leave dried food for her in the scullery of the house
where a window had been left open, but autumn gales had made
it impossible for her to continue to do this and they feared for
the cat. We, of course, 240 miles away, could do nothing to
help, as Babs's resignation did not take effect until the end of
the Christmas term. It seemed impossible that the cat could
survive, although rumour had it that she had been seen fishing
off the rocks. If this were so, she must have been a very
remarkable cat. Remarkable she was, for survive she did. The
Whitehouses left in August and we did not take up residence
until February. On each of our forays with furniture during

January and early February we had left several plates of dried
food, water and milk for her as Toni Whitehouse had done.
Always on our return all the dishes were empty but one.
However long the intervals between our visits there was always
one dish left in reserve. Surely even non-cat lovers must realize
that only a superior intelligence would leave an iron ration in
reserve for emergency. Not once, however, had she revealed
herself and so it was now. Each night we left food and drink for
her in the scullery and by morning it had gone. For many weeks
there was no sign of her in person; silently and mysteriously she
came and went. But that she was watching our every move was
later revealed in a most uncanny fashion. Meantime we
continued to provide for our invisible guest.

Having done so that night, Ruth, Toby and I retired to bed,
this time, more conventionally, in a bedroom, because before
daylight faded we had dragged some mattresses upstairs. The
house is situated on a promontory and on one side the front door
is not more than ten yards from the cliff edge. The house appears
to be built on rock; and one hopes that this is so, for the
Whitehouses said that during their stay they had lost eight feet
of pathway from this very edge, due to a landside. Another eight
feet would be periliously near to the front door. One of my early
fears was that one morning I would step straight out of the door,
over the cliff edge to the sea below. One soon learns to be
philosophical however; more pertinent hazards jostle out the
fanciful ones and one tries to harness a fervid imagination to a
practical use. In any case the joys of living on an island far
outweigh the dangers and disadvantages, the discomfort and
sometimes sheer physical misery. This is difficult to explain to
those who have never succumbed to the lure of islands (or
mountains, with which they are akin); but it is true that once an
island casts its spell one is held in thrall. Willingly, challenges
are met head-on; pitting one's wits against the difficulties
thrown at one by nature and machinery becomes a way of life,
and the physical discomforts are endured for the ineffable joy of
living in an enchanted, magical world.

So it seemed that night as I looked out of the window of the bare bedroom, across the moonlit sea to Eddystone lighthouse flashing its friendly light twelve and a half miles away. I drifted off to sleep to the roar of the surf on the rocks below, and I exulted in my good fortune, only sad that Babs would be resting her head in the cottage on the mainland and would be regretting, too, that we were not together to share these rare and exciting experiences.

As the sun streamed through the windows next morning, our first Monday on the island, we lit the fire to make coffee and discussed plans for the day. Ruth had been detailed by Wren to rub down the buoy ready for mooring our boat the *Islander*. The buoy, a massive lump of rusting metal, looked more like a wartime mine washed up by the sea, and Ruth was welcome to this task. I opted to take another look at the generator. It seemed important to the smooth running of our lives to overcome the burdensome chore of making the twice nightly pilgrimage, first to swing it into action, then later to silence it so that we could retire to bed. As those who have followed our earlier adventures will know, I am not enamoured of machinery. On the contrary I have an almost pathological fear of it and of engines that leap into apparently uncontrollable life at the touch of a switch or lever. I have never had the least desire to subdue them to my bidding and have always been more than happy to leave even the driving of a car to others more eager than myself. Nevertheless it seemed desirable to come to terms with some of these monsters if we were to survive with a modicum of comfort.

If I had known then how much our lives were to be dominated by machinery in all its fiendish forms, and subject to its most malevolent moods, I might never have set foot on this particular island, but made hotfoot for a desert island where fire would have to be conjured up by rubbing two sticks together, and a light obtained, if I remember rightly from childhood reading, by igniting a brazil nut — of all things! I knew for certain that I should have to live with the generator, for Babs — a car driver — who, one assumed, would have at least a working knowledge of the mysteries lying under the bonnet, and should not therefore be daunted by wheels and cogs and things that whirred and spluttered, would be living on the mainland for the greater part of the time, and Ruth, who revelled in things mechanical, would be leaving in two or three months time. Resolutely, therefore, I entered the generator-room and read the instruction book. 'If engine fails to start, locate N and M. Press reset in case K has tripped.' It read like a piece of spy fiction. Who were the sinister N and M? and had K really fallen for their wiles? Or perhaps MI5 was responsible but was too secret to be mentioned!

Hastily I retreated. Wren was right, it was a job for the Lister engineer. So off I went to the beach to collect driftwood and seaweed. We had been told that potatoes grow particularly well on seaweed and it seemed a matter of some urgency to plant some as soon as possible. The island has an exceptionally mild climate, similar, we had been told, to that of the Isles of Scilly; also, that produce was a month ahead of Hannafore, only one mile opposite on the mainland. The general saying, too, was that one layer of clothing less was needed on the island than in Looe. Being surrounded by sea the island rarely has frost, and snow is so uncommon we have only seen it three times in the twenty years we have been here. On each occasion it was a mere sprinkling and disappeared before the day was out. This is astonishing, for in Looe, every winter, frost and ice make the roads dangerous, and it is a regular feature for the steep hills rising out of Looe to be gritted to make them passable, and Babs has frequently had to deal with an iced-up car. This was a common occurrence at Epsom Downs, our former home, and an accepted hazard of our long winters there.

So it has never ceased to be a wonder to us that our new home enjoys a sub-tropical climate. Honeysuckle blooms around the porch at Christmastide and it has become an established tradition with us to gather as many garden and wild flowers as we can to make a Christmas garland. Usually we can reckon on picking at least thirty varieties, including sweet-smelling violets which bloom in the woods from November to March. In the warmth of our short winters growth is rapid too. Whereas we were accustomed to sowing biennials in the autumn to flower the following spring, we found that by following this practice on the island, plants would come up in a matter of weeks and be in full flower the whole of the winter right through to summer. On a January day it is a glorious sight to look out of the window and see the borders a blaze of colour from the many-hued wallflowers and stock, soon to be followed by fields of daffodils. Before winter is scarce departed the woods become a sea of primroses and bluebells and we feel that St George's is indeed one of the 'Fortunate Isles'. All this we were yet to find out.

We had been told that it was tradition to plant early potatoes on Boxing Day. As it was now February it seemed a matter of urgency to sow them as soon as possible and I was determined to get started at once. That second morning, therefore, with the house in utter chaos, I spent carting wheelbarrow-loads of seaweed up from the shore-line to a field near the house. I then dug a long trench, lined it with seaweed, covered this with a layer of beautiful friable soil, which we knew from having tested it previously to be almost 100 per cent loam and slightly alkaline, then planted Arran Pilot seed potatoes in the prepared trench. On one of our brief trips over Wren had announced, because of the stormy seas, 'Hand luggage only!' For some obscure reason potatoes seemed to fill the bill and subsequently we staggered through the surf with a sackful apiece of seed potatoes, and frantically chitted them out in the twenty minutes we were allowed ashore. On another trip in January we had spent our precious time digging a field at breakneck speed as though our lives depended on it, planting as many as we could in the time. I do not recall why potato planting was such an obsession with us. We had never bothered to grow them previously; tomatoes, runner beans and lettuce being the extent of our culinary ambitions. Always flirting with diets, our own intake of potatoes had been a modest seven-pound pack to last the whole winter, potatoes being unfashionable with the diet-conscious at that time. This near-mania for sowing them, then, can only be attributed to the seductive appeal of producing a crop way ahead of ordinary mainland mortals. A local greengrocer had offered

us 3s. 6d. a pound for any earlies we could produce, so we knew
the island seaweed-grown potatoes were a highly desirable crop,
for 3s. 6d. was a very high price indeed in 1965, especially as
this was the wholesale price.

Alas! for these grandiose schemes. That year a blight ruined
the nation's crop and the field we planted suffered the same fate,
but for some reason this particular brave little row escaped and
by May produced the largest and most delectable potatoes we
had ever tasted. This was the general consensus of opinion, too,
as we handed them out like a rare and exotic fruit, and with the
overweening pride of inordinately proud parents. We sowed
more than potatoes that day for we planted with them an
interest that has flourished and multiplied over the years.
Nowadays I dig hundreds of feet of trenches; we drag up
truck-loads of seaweed and line the trenches with this and
comfrey plus our own compost from the many heaps which we
build. Over the years we have grown dozens of different
varieties. These seed potatoes we obtain from Donald Maclean
of Crieff, Perthshire, the acknowledged doyen of the potato
world. He cultivates some 359 different varieties (the figure
given for 1985) and he will sell them in small quantities, even as
few as two or four tubers of the rarer ones, to those who wish to
experiment. We so desire and I keep charts and analyse the data
to find the best kinds for our soil and climate, and we hold
potato tastings to judge the flavour and texture. Two of our
voluntary helpers, Jim and Barbara Chanter, in addition to
chopping logs for our winter fires and helping our conservation
project in many useful ways, lift our main-crop potatoes. They
plump for 'Vanessa'. Clarrie, who, with her friend Betty —
both retired agricultural college lecturers — comes to help
every year, favours 'Estima'. She takes a penknife from her
pocket and with a deft flick of her wrist will delicately shave the
merest wisp of skin from her chosen 'Estima' to reveal with some
triumph the golden flesh beneath. Mesmerized I watch, as
before my eyes, she transforms the humble spud to a gleaming
jewel, waving her penknife much as a conjuror waves his wand.
We give the gold award to 'Bintje', The 'Duke of York' ties

for silver with 'Estima'. 'Romano' gets the bronze. However, there are many more for us to try, and experiments to make.

This operation took the whole of that first Monday morning, for in addition to the lengthy task of digging the trench and lugging up seaweed I had to locate the trays of seed potatoes. It may seem incredible that two large trays of potatoes could go missing but the truth was that our early days were bedevilled by a complete inability to find *anything*. The nature of our moves over, in rough seas in mid-winter, meant that all our belongings had been piled indiscriminately in the hall and kitchen of the house. Imminent storms forced hurried retreats to the boat to make the safety of Looe harbour, and each succeeding trip only added to the chaos. On one unexpected calm crossing in early February — a summer-like day — we had attempted to make a slight clearance by removing some of our goods and chattels down to the large room leading off from Jetty Cottage. This room which was a converted barn, and had at one time been a music room, we designated as a transit camp and hoped to mount it as our operations room and restore some sort of order out of the chaos. It was a mammoth task, however, and we only had time even on this less frantic of our visits to move a few of the more cumbersome of our possessions, as a wheelbarrow was our only means of transport. At least we could just get into the house and make a passage through the hall to the lounge where we had slept on that first memorable night and where we now cooked our meals over the driftwood fire.

You would think that coming from a compact modern house, we would have plenty of room on an island for all our worldly goods. Although from the outside Island House looks large, a mansion dominating the cliffs above Jetty Bay — some visitors wonder why we do not use it as an hotel — it is in fact just two up and two down: two bedrooms above and, below, a large lounge and a farmhouse kitchen, flanked by a wide hall. All three are oak-beamed and the hall and kitchen as well as the adjoining scullery are stone-flagged. Half-way up the stairs is a large bathroom supported by outhouses below and crowned with a flat roof nestling below the gables of the house. This flat roof would make an ideal observatory, for with no town or city lights to dim the stars and no air pollution it would be a perfect location for the study of astronomy. With this in mind, but at present only a dream, we have acquired quite an extensive library on this subject.

In searching for the elusive trays of seed potatoes I pounced with triumph among the mountains of artefacts on a log saw. On our many moves from Epsom Downs we usually stayed overnight with friends of ours, Jack and Betty MacAllister, who at that time lived in Newton Poppleford in Devon. Jack had presented us with this brand new saw as he reckoned that our need would be greater than his. A thoughtful gift, for although I had no intention of taking up pickaxing as a retirement activity, I conjectured, and rightly, that sawing would be a most useful skill to acquire in our new life. And so it was and still is. Never a hatchet or chopper lady, a saw seems to lend itself to my particular style. It is the rhythmic movement that appeals more than the clashing cymbal-like action required to chop and hack. Whatever the reason we have, over the years, acquired an impressive array of saws. The names alone have often persuaded us to buy them. A coping saw, surely, is one to give confidence whatever the challenge; and a rip saw, what better one to use if one were feeling in a fine carefree mood! Often have I wondered how we could ever live without the support of, for instance, a tenon saw — the euphony of the word alone opens up whole new vistas of gracious living.

This log saw was the first and one of the most valued of our collection, and many has been the time when I have silently thanked Jack, who, unfortunately, is no longer with us, for his contribution to our island life. It seemed a good idea, now that I had this newly found treasure, to saw up some wood ready for the evening fire.

Driftwood fires sound romantic to those who depend on central heating or gas or electric fires, and so they are. There is nothing to compare with sitting snugly in front of one on a stormy winter's night, the blazing logs sending out a rich warmth and assailing one's nostrils with aromatic delight. As with all pleasures, however, especially those of an island, there is a price to pay. Of all open fires a driftwood fire has a voracious appetite. It is all too easy to fall into the trap of spending the greater part of each day collecting wood and sawing it in order to have enough to burn at night.

There was no danger of this happening today, for having found the saw I promptly lost it again. Re-losing found objects seems to be an occupational hazard here. Short of slinging everything for the day around one's neck there is no answer except to lead a tidier life or cut down one's activities to single figures. How many hobbies have the houseproud? If they have any they would definitely not be the messy types where impedimenta is strewn all over the place. Perhaps the answer is to live in a confined space, like a sailor in his cabin, for how true it is, like Parkinson's Law, that the more space there is the more one will find to fill it.

On that first working day it hit me between the eyes that to achieve anything at all without spending valuable time searching for and losing everything again, some sort of order must be made out of the chaos in the kitchen. Over lunch of toasted cheese sandwich, made over the driftwood fire and helped enormously by quaffs of peach wine Tokay 1962, I persuaded Ruth, who was hell bent on scraping rust off the buoy, that we really must sort things out a bit. Supposedly it would have been the first thing a housewife would have set about, but neither of us was a housewife by training, inclination or choice. On the other hand I doubt if a dedicated housewife would have allowed herself to get into this situation in the first place. However, one has to do chores, even in paradise; so reluctantly, that afternoon, we began to push some of the furniture out into the hall. If we had known that we could not run the deep freeze from the generator we had then and had for many years to come, we might even have pushed it over the cliff, but by moving it into the hall we had some walking space in the kitchen.

Soon it was time to go down to the main beach for an assignation to wave to Babs over on the mainland. While awaiting her we collected more driftwood that had been tossed up by the afternoon tide. At last I espied her through the binoculars, a lonely figure on the rocks at Hannafore. Somehow she looked pathetic and it was with a great sense of loneliness that I watched her wave, turn and climb back over the rocks.

Ruth and I had managed to drag a couple of bedsteads upstairs by moonlight, so that night we slept in great luxury, Toby thankfully sharing my bed. So far he had not accompanied me on any of my expeditions and when I did lure him outside he had hurriedly retreated. Even the calls of nature were dealt with quickly and quietly. Although I accompanied him, these sorties were no farther than was strictly necessary, then back we had to come to the comfort of his new home. He was, after all, thirteen and a half years old with a heart condition, and, like all pets, he was very conservative. These habits persisted for a considerable time. We were perplexed, and worried that he would not get enough exercise and that being an islander did not suit him after all. We need not have been concerned. Having established his roots he gradually extended his territory and eventually the whole island became his domain.

That night I revelled in the luxury of a comfortable bed and as again I drifted off to sleep by moonlight the world seemed a good place.

The next day it dawned on me that although we were civilized to the extent that we had actually undressed and slept in nighties in proper beds, this was Tuesday; we had not had a wash since Saturday morning on the mainland, and we had been completely unaware of the fact. Frantically I looked for my toothbrush. Having at last located it I performed my ablutions with water from the hot-water bottle, as water from the tap was giving off most unpleasant effluvia. A change of clothing seemed desirable but here again it was difficult to locate any. Incredible as it may seem I spent the rest of the day half-clothed in the few items I could find, secure in the knowledge that there was no one to see me except Ruth, Toby and the gulls. When we at last ventured out for our perpetual search for driftwood my anorak enveloped me in its comforting warmth and gave me an illusion of respectability — so far! In restrospect it seemed a far cry from the days so recently relinquished when I commuted daily to London, rising to the personal challenge that I must face each day in a different outfit and bedecked with earrings, matching lapel brooch, discreetly elegant ring and an immaculate hair style crowned with a hat — a 'must' in those days for anyone with any self-respect. Casual clothes were for weekends only but chosen equally carefully with an eye to colour and suitability. Perhaps suitability is the key to the metamorphosis that this short taste of island life had brought about. Hand-tailored suits and stylish outfits may have been mandatory in my former life, but the island demanded jeans, oilskins, sea boots and anoraks and happily I bowed to its dictates. The anorak that only partially covered my half-clad figure that day has passed into history, for patched and mended many times by Babs — for I have no skill with a needle — I still don it thankfully each winter for the worst of the outside jobs.

Thus clad, Ruth and I, accompanied by Toby, who was persuaded to come if I put his lead on, made our pilgrimage to the generator room. To our consternation the generator would not start. Reference to all the important charts suggested that the air-filter might need cleaning. While Ruth was trying to locate this I found that Toby had disappeared, lead and all. Worried beyond belief I dashed up to the house to find that the heavy door has been pushed open, but of Toby there was no sign. Frantically I called him. I called again. After a long pause there was a faint and distant 'Woof! Woof!' from above. He had taken himself to bed. I took some peach wine down to Ruth for it seemed to me that a bit of stimulus would help fathom the mysteries of filthy filters and the like. And so it was. The filter suitably cleaned according to the instructions, the generator was away and once more we had electricity.

Close by the generator room is the tractor shed. This is a large brick building which houses a tractor, a plough, an assortment of farm machinery and all manner of garden equipment and unidentifiable ironmongery — some of this last seemingly dating back to the last century. This highlights another problem of island life. How do you dispose of articles that have outlived their usefulness, if they are not burnable, for the dustmen never call? This we have never satisfactorily solved. Neither apparently, had the previous owners, judging by the bric-à-brac, obsolete machinery and kitchen equipment that cluttered the many outhouses. One blackened metal jug caught my eye. It was almost certainly a Victorian hot-water-jug. In spite of its neglected condition it had a nice line and sense of balance. Over the years I grew fond of it, blackened as it was, and took it up to the house several times meaning to clean it, but somehow never got around to doing so. A few years later one of our helpers, a young graduate, knowing of my interest, bought himself some cleaning pads, and secretly spent every evening cleaning and polishing it. One morning there appeared on our doorstep a gleaming brass hot-water jug, burnished with loving care, by Julian, and transformed into an article of real beauty. The following year we saw a similar one in an antique shop. It was smaller and rather battered. It was priced at £28. At today's prices it would probably be worth considerably more.

This day, however, I seized on a treasure that made me shout with delight — a tin bath. Triumphantly I dragged it up to the house, filled it with rain-water and heated it over the log fire. Fortunately the fireplace, made from island rock, is very large and in olden days would have been used for spit-roasting. We now had a field day. First we washed all our cooking utensils, then our clothes, and finally ourselves, with, I hasten to add, a change of rain-water between each operation. It is surprising how luxurious and comforting it is to have a bath in front of a roaring log fire and I was reminded, as I so often am, after returning from some bruising and sometimes bloody expedition, of Rupert Brooke's 'benediction of hot water'.

Greatly refreshed, I decided to explore the island. There had been little time to do so since our arrival for we had been fully occupied with our battle for survival. The extent of our exploration had been to penetrate the jungle of our possessions in search of some vital object, and our forages no farther than to the generator room or down the path to the main beach in the inevitable search for driftwood. Not that the island is big, but its topography makes it appear larger than it is. Only twenty-two and a half acres in extent and about a mile in circumference it is possible nevertheless for the island to hide anyone's whereabouts for hours, even when just a stroll is involved. Many islands are barren and treeless. St George's, unlike most small islands, is wooded. It is 150 feet high and hilly in every direction. In fact there is only one piece of land which is level, a lawn at the back of the house, and it is man-made, having being levelled and shored up by dry-stone walls. This, in its former glory, was a croquet lawn — a delightful game we had both enjoyed in our youth — but alas! we have so far found no time for it in our busy lives here.

The island's illusion of size is enhanced by the indented coastline, a labyrinth of caves, rocky coves and steeply rising cliffs. The western seaboard is like a Land's End in miniature; exposed to the full fury of the westerly gales that roar in from the Atlantic, its rocky cliffs jut out into the broiling sea below, which never seems calm on that side of the island. From the summit one looks westward past Hoare Stone to Gribben Head with Mevagissey and Dodman Point beyond. On a very clear day it is possible to see the Lizard Peninsula, and it gives one a feeling of immensity and a sense of being part of the universe to realize that beyond the horizon the first landfall would be South America with perchance a glance at the Azores on the way. It is a very steep and often dangerous climb down to the caves below, in one of which, we were told, a silver sword was found before the war.

It was up to the top that I climbed today. Behind me just below the summit nestled a field protected on three sides by woods and bramble. It is here that the first daffodils, 'Magnificence', appear. Usually they begin to bloom in January, but they were late this year and today I had my first sight of them, and I knew that one of our first island activities was about to begin. We had been told that fifteen varieties of daffodils were grown on the island, five acres being under cultivation. This is not instantly apparent for, except when the daffodils are in bloom from January to March, the fields are verdant, the grass apparently giving some protection against the gales. Visitors who come in the summer when the daffodil bulbs are dormant see only what they think is lush meadowland divided by luxuriant hedges of mauve veronica and pink escallonia. 'Why', they demand, to our constant irritation, 'do you not keep sheep and cows?' Some remain unconvinced even when we explain that if we had the expertise, time and inclination we should have to give up the daffodil farm, for not only would the blooms be trampled upon but they would be poisonous to livestock. Farmers, of course, never ask us. It is usually those from urban areas, who when motoring through the countryside see the apparently idyllic sight of sheep and cows grazing on farmland. In the past I had a friend who was a farmer, and seeing at first hand the ills and disasters that can beset livestock, I was convinced that this was not the kind of life that I could happily share or one of which I could make a success. I knew, too, that however much of a strain teaching was at times, Babs's thoughts had never turned to sheep and cows as an antidote. Neither of us had, of course, ever during our careers yearned for a daffodil farm, but this was a *fait accompli*, and although we were well aware of our ignorance, and had moments of trepidation, in our more optimistic moods we told ourselves that it was nothing more than a glorified garden on a grand scale. That there was much more to it than that we were about to find out.

Excited that soon we should be harvesting our first daffodils I quickly skirted the woods and descended by the steep track to the south-eastern tip of the island and across the narrow footbridge to the 'Little Island'. From the peninsula the 'Little Island' points like a finger south-east past Rame Head to Prawle Point in Devon. In all directions gulls wheeled and screamed. In a full gale they will ride the wind; one after another they will rise on the eddies and gusts and gracefully dip down again. This will go on for hours and it is quite hypnotic to watch them. Was, perhaps, the inventor of the Yo-Yo inspired by gulls?

I did not stay to explore the 'Little Island' for I had another assignation with Babs to wave to her on the mainland, but although I looked carefully through the binoculars from the main beach, there was no sign of her at all. Despondently I began to pick up driftwood when, to my astonishment, I saw our boat the *Islander* leaving the harbour—a lone craft in that expanse of sea. Soon there was great excitement for in addition to Babs and Wren, Ruth's mother Mrs Jennings, Mrs Whitehouse, her son Desmond and our two schoolboy helpers, Charles and Duncan, stepped out of the boat.

Babs brought with her a wonderful assortment of food — chicken, pork chops, vegetables, apples, chocolate, bread and most important of all — fresh water. Soon our lounge was alive with the buzz of conversation. To show the measure of their concern for us everyone spent the whole time telling us what to do until my head was spinning. That night I went to sleep to the relentless rhythm of 'What you should do is . . . What you should do is . . .' pounding through my head. It is a litany that has gone on over the years. Hardly a visitor sets foot here without telling us what we ought to do. If we did all the things suggested we should certainly not have any time for visitors! Imagine a farmer waiting at the farmhouse door to welcome visitors and entertaining them to tea during the sowing or harvesting season, or breaking off milking the cows or shearing the sheep to answer questions about farming life and and what it is like in the winter!

The next morning, our first Wednesday on the island, we again filled our new-found treasure, the tin bath, with rain-water, heated it on the open fire, and luxuriated in the bliss of a bath — island style. It seems extraordinary in retrospect but I remember deciding that this operation, necessary and enjoyable as it was, took up too much time, and any further ablutions, I said, must wait until the weekend!

Around lunch-time we noticed that suddenly the sea had almost disappeared between us and Hannafore. Unbeknown to us this was one of the biggest spring tides of the year when high and low water are at their highest and lowest. Traditionally on Good Friday it is possible to walk across from the mainland dry-shod. Over the years, however, we have noticed that this exceptional spring tide is variable and may occur either in February or March. It is only possible to walk across if it is calm, which it rarely is at this time of year. Even then one has only minutes to spare to make the return trip. It is quite frightening to be slithering on the seaweed-strewn rocks, in the middle of the channel, with the sea rapidly encroaching on either side. It takes little imagination to realize that if one should slip the future could be very bleak indeed, and that within a very short space of time the sea would be many feet above one, and increasing to a fathomless amount with the racing tide. No wonder many locals say that they have never attempted the trip across. Today there was no question of walking across; the sea was running swiftly and deeply through the only possible channel. The rapidly receding tide revealed a mass of menacing rocks between us and Hannafore and gave the extraordinary effect that the island was rising out of the sea. It seemed an excellent opportunity to do a survey of the rocks and sea-bed, and so chart a passage for our boat. In my ignorance I did not realize that the winter seas have a tremendous effect on the state of the beaches and sea-bed. Cliffs of shingle thrown up by a storm from one direction will be obliterated and replaced by a vast expanse of sand from an onshore gale. A north-west squall will drive sand in one's face, stinging it raw, so that it's like floundering in the Sahara in a sandstorm, albeit a frozen one. A south-east gale will sweep away the sand, revealing rocks that have not been seen for years.

Happily unaware of these dramatic changes in the topography, I had a quick glass of peach wine, pulled on my seaboots and, with a notebook and camera, waded as far into the middle of the channel as I could. Even as I stood there sketching, the wind changed with the turn of the tide and freshened from the east, a direction hated by the local fishermen. With the sea now rolling rapidly in on either side it seemed prudent to return to the shore. It was as exciting as my mountaineering days when one stood on a peak in danger of being enveloped by swirling mists which had risen from nowhere, making it hazardous and sometimes impossible to find the path down to the valley, and one was in danger of being benighted unless the mist lifted. Now, though, the path was quite clear — back to the beach as soon as possible. From high up on the beach I took photos of the now fast-disappearing rocks. Soon the mainland receded, almost as though the island had set sail and soon one would be in mid-Atlantic. This is an illusion that persists to this day and is further heightened by the fact that the island, except for its two beaches, rises perpendicular from the sea. The house, which stands on the cliff top, has a bathroom with magnificent views in three directions and is like the bridge of a ship. When the seas sweep past below one can almost feel the movement as though the island were riding the waves. This impression is so vivid that we keep a compass in the bathroom to check the direction of the wind, although it is patently obvious that the points of the compass do not change.

After my charting expedition I reluctantly returned to the mundane task of clearing out the kitchen. In a few hours it became quite habitable but there was no way we could get the Aga to start. As it was all rusted up from lying idle for six months in the damp sea atmosphere and the wet days of autumn and winter, there was only one solution that we could see; dismantle it as much as possible and scrape off the rust. This we did, taking any parts we could detach on to the lawn outside the front door. We scrubbed industriously with wire brushes in the most incongruous setting imaginable. There we were on a cliff top, a couple of veritable Cinderellas, up to our elbows in rust and dirt, our faces smudged with soot. We scraped away at these assorted bits of ironmongery, in clouds of rust, to the accompaniment of the roar of the sea below and the haunting cries of the seagulls, their wings flashing in the sunlight. Around us golden daffodils were appearing everywhere, belying the fact that it was mid-February. Beyond, the green seas raced past the island from the east, white horses riding the crest of the waves and sparkling in the sunlight. Encouraged, no doubt, by the setting, not to mention the ubiquitous peach wine, we worked with a will. I blessed the greengrocer, back in Banstead in Surrey, who had let me have crates of over-ripe peaches at 2s. 6d. a crate, for I was able to bring several demijohns of this golden nectar to the island. In no time at all the Aga bits and pieces were polished bright, and reassembled. We would, however, need some charcoal to ignite the fuel, and I hoped that Babs would bring some on her next trip.

Her half-term holiday was due the coming weekend, so the next priority now that the kitchen was more or less habitable was to get the flagstaff in working order in readiness for her arrival. For some reason it seemed essential—although we had more pressing problems, such as the putrid water that still gushed out of the taps — that we get the St George's flag flying so that we could greet Babs in style. Babs and I are very proud of this flag. We inherited it with other island accoutrements, together with another flag which we were told you used if you required a doctor. Mr Whitehouse told us that the idea was that you lay it out on the boathouse roof. One of the stories that Mrs Whitehouse told us was that they had arranged a signal with a friend of theirs who lived over at Hannafore whereby they would put a white sheet on the boathouse roof as an invitation to tea. The coastguard mistook this for the medical SOS and sent the lifeboat out! We have sometimes wondered during the time I was alone on the island how it would be possible to stagger down to the beach, climb up to the roof of the boathouse, and put the flag there if one were so ill that medical aid was required — and who would see it supposing these acrobatics *were* performed if it were dead of night or there was a thick sea mist?

But as usual there were more pertinent problems to be dealt with without worrying about hypothetical ones. We were told that we were allowed officially to fly the St George's flag, a privilege, we understood, accorded to Admirals of the Fleet and Church of England churches. In some guide books the tale goes that in a sea battle of long ago, Looe, then a port, sent twenty-one ships of the line, second only to the number from London. The battleship St George did so well that St Michael's Island, as it was then called, was renamed St George's Island.

We have copies of old maps dated 1588, the year of the Armada, giving the title St Michael's. Present-day large-scale maps give it as St George's or Looe Island. Naturally we favour St George's. The Vatican may say St George is no longer a saint but he still represents England, and with great ceremony each year on 23 April we celebrate St George's Day and Shakespeare's birthday by hoisting the flag and drinking a toast in island wine. In wine-making circles, traditionally, dandelion wine is made on 23 April. Weather permitting, as part of the celebrations, we do so too, and drink of this delectable nectar, if there is any left from the previous year. It is a fancy of mine that one year we will have actors performing parts of *Henry V* on top of the island, with visitors en masse contributing to the crowd scenes. How appropriate on 23 April it would be to hear the rousing words from Act III, Scene 1:

> Follow your spirit, and upon this charge
> Cry *'God for Harry, England, and Saint George!'*

Unfortunately on this day although we had a flag there was no flagpole. On the cliffs on the south-east promontory of the island, above the bridge leading to Little Island, stood a tabernacle; this is a kind of socket made of three pieces of timber sunk in the ground, bound with iron bands and standing some four feet high. This made a receptable for the flagpole. There were, in fact, two tabernacles, one quite rotten from years of weathering. In course of time we were to discover why there was no flagpole — it is impossible for any to survive the winter storms for long. Over the years we have lost several and a year or so ago, during a particularly violent storm, the tremendous seas broke right over the cliff top. The tabernacle itself was uprooted and swept by the sea to the cliff edge on the other side of the promontory. Inexplicably it was the sound one that went and the semi-rotten one has come into its own again, serving us in good stead right up to the present time. As I write the current flagpole has a slightly drunken list to starboard, the result of an early autumn gale, auguring ill for its survival this coming winter. On this day we were lucky enough to find a very tall post in the sweet pea area of the Smugglers' Garden, which we thought might do, and a hunt among the treasures in the tractor shed produced a pulley. Eventually after many abortive attempts we managed to hoist the flag. Satisfied that we could greet Babs in appropriate style when the time came, we hauled it down, dismantled the precious pole, and returned to the house to clear a space in the bedroom for her.

On Saturday, just one week after our historic landing, about the time when Babs was due, Ruth and I marched out to the cliff top in a biting blizzard, with the pole perched on our shoulders, for all the world looking like a clip from a Laurel and Hardy film. We managed to slot the pole into the tabernacle and attached the flag to the rope. Expectantly I stood by ready to hoist it as soon as we spotted the *Islander*. Earlier we had noted a great swell coming in from the east. Now it was racing in, crested with white horses. This meant that there would be a 'bar' in the river mouth, making it difficult or perhaps impossible for any vessel to leave the harbour.

I trained the binoculars on the harbour mouth. There was not a boat in sight; indeed there was not a sign of craft anywhere at sea. Anxiously I scanned the road above the rocks at Hannafore in case Babs should be there to give a signal. Suddenly I espied her blue anorak and the unexpected sight of our Mini with the fibre-glass dinghy aloft. So they were going to row across the 'Island Roads'—the channel between the island and Hannafore. This would be some expedition; not only was Babs coming with stores, but friends of ours from Surrey, Brian and Anne Rainforth and their two young children, were to stay with us, for it was Brian's half-term holiday also, for he, too, was a teacher. Hastily I hoisted the flag, which stuck at half-mast at the first attempt. An evil omen, I thought grimly, but after a few furious tugs from us both it made it to the top. We then raced down to the beach leaving the flag flying defiantly and bravely in the now blustering wind. At last we could see Wren rowing Anne and the children across in the little white craft. Meantime Babs and Brian were climbing down over the treacherous rocks on the other side, loaded with stores and luggage. The plan was,

Wren told us, that having landed Anne and the children, he would row back in our larger metal boat, to bring over the other two and all the gear. We all lent a hand to get the heavy metal boat down to the shore to launch it. Eventually everything and everyone were safely across the racing tide, high but not dry, for they were all soaked to the skin from spray and lopping waves. No one appeared to be worried about this and our little party, loaded with stores and luggage, made its way up to the house. Excitement was so great no one gave a thought to changing into dry clothes. Proudly, on the way up to the house, we showed Brian the generator. Oozing sea water, he nevertheless was greatly impressed, although he had very little chance to appear otherwise. It must be said, for the record, that even after all these years, the generator is still our own little bit of magic. We never cease to marvel that (when once it became fully functional) at the flick of an ordinary light-switch anywhere on the island, it will leap into life and the whole island will, in the immortal words, be 'lit up'. Sad to say the magic does not always work, but then, does any magic? Or, come to that, does any machinery?

Babs and I went out to the flagpole and ceremoniously hauled down the flag. As dusk was fast approaching Wren and Ruth took their leave, for Ruth was to spend a few days with her parents while Babs was with me. They rowed back to the mainland in the fibre-glass dinghy, with the trolley for hauling it over the rocks at Hannafore perched aloft, and a weird craft it made it look. We then entertained our guests to a slap-up meal — island style — of eggs, bacon and baked beans; the driftwood fire adding its own subtle aroma. Eventually, after much talk and laughter, we retired. Babs, bless her heart, was very impressed with the bedroom. The fact that she had a proper bed to lie on and sheets to sleep between would seem to her, no doubt, the height of luxury after her first night on bare boards. There was certainly nothing else in the bedroom for her to admire, for it was otherwise quite bare. The others bedded down in Jetty Cottage in some fashion or other.

The following day we set about trying to get some of the more important things in order. Babs had brought some charcoal with her, and our de-rusting efforts must have been effective for she had the Aga going in no time at all. Since that day it has become the heart of the island. The constant heat transforms the kitchen from the lifeless shell we found to a place of warmth and friendliness that seems to envelop all who enter. It appears to exert a magnetism, for young and old alike are drawn to it and bask in its warmth even in the height of summer. Appreciatively they sniff the tantalizing smells, and they say that there is just something about it that makes them want to loiter awhile. Maybe it is the fragrance of newly-baked bread, mingling with the headiness of fermenting wine. The sight of gallons of brilliantly clear wine in the demijohns stacked in racks from the stone-flagged floor to the oak-beamed ceiling has an irresistible appeal, with perhaps the hope of island hospitality to come. It is not only that, for the kitchen has the same attraction for little ones of four years' old and non-drinkers alike. We, too, feel the same and are never happier than when we are pottering about there immersed in our many activities. This is strange, for it is the only room on the island that has no view. One door leads to the scullery, the other into the hall; a third wall houses the enormous Aga, cupboards, shelving and the like. Only the fourth wall has windows. These certainly are large, and pierce the side of the house whose walls are three to four feet thick, but they look out to a high bank, beyond which hedges and fields slope steeply up to the woods, masking any views, for the house is actually cut into the hillside. It is cosy in the depth of winter, when the wind is howling and the island is lashed by storms, to sit at the kitchen table making our various crafts, or to have a bake-up. There would be no view anyway, for the windows everywhere are generally thick with sea-spray which flies over the top of the house, falling in scuds of foam, covering the lawn beyond like a carpet of snow. This is peeping into the future, for at that time we had been on the island just a week, with many daunting tasks to tackle before we could indulge in the making of crafts, enjoy and have the satisfaction of baking, or bask in the ineffable luxury of just sitting. Suffice

it was that we had the Aga going and one could say that the heart
of the island was beginning to beat again.

The next imperative task was to tackle the problem of the
water supply. We had previously inspected the two
water-storage tanks in the woods and had made an abortive
attempt to clear out the stinking weeds growing in them. Now
on lifting the lid and looking more closely we found that a tree
was actually growing in the outlet pipe. First we emptied out all
the stagnating water. Brian then cleaned it out while we drained
all the water from the tanks and pipes in the house and cottages.
After a good 'do' with the sodium chlorate in the offending
tanks we went down to the jetty beach and climbed the steps up
to the door in the cliff face. Within was the petrol pump. This
we managed to start, which was remarkable considering that it
had not been used since last summer and would be damp from
its close proximity to the sea which had been pounding at the
steps a few feet below all winter long. During that day and the
next we continued to pump water into the tanks and run it out
of the taps in the dwellings to flush out the system. By the end
of the second day, although there was still a faint smell, we
decided that the water was good enough for washing, so daily
ablutions were now added to our curriculum. If any of the smell
clung to our skin, we were of the opinion that we were all in the
same boat, so to speak, and would not notice each other — we
hoped.

After a day or two more of pumping and emptying we held a
committee meeting, and issued the 'Flushing Report'. For,
greatly daring, we had been sipping it at intervals, and when
the taste of the sodium chlorate had disappeared, and nobody
had actually collapsed, we decided that it was now good enough
to drink. Presumably we boiled the water as an added
precaution, but after this lapse of time I do not remember. I
rather doubt it, for one of the effects of island life is that one
begins to live dangerously in some ways, at least by mainland
standards. A casual insouciance creeps into one's attitude
towards matters that would be quite unacceptable in a more
sophisticated society. This does not mean that our standards are

necessarily lower, but they are different. When you live close to
nature you have to get your priorities right, and fussiness over
food and drink gives way to thankfulness that you have any at
all. Only gradually were we able to substitute our own island
standards of good wholesome food, grown without poisonous
chemicals, for our previous brand of fastidiousness. Some
whims were discarded instantly.

Coffee was a case in point. In my previous civilized existence
coffee was of supreme importance. For me there were only two
acceptable beans: one was a Kenya coffee bean from the Army
and Navy Stores; the other, freshly roasted beans from the
Algerian shop in Soho. After a long day in the office I would
dash up to Soho and arrive home late in the evening clutching
my precious parcel, the delicious aroma of the beans — still
warm from roasting — assailing one's nostrils and full of
'Eastern Promise' of the delights to come. I would then
hand-grind the beans and serve coffee *à la filtre* to everyone.
Both jug and cups had to be thick brown earthenware: the
delectable flavour and the fragrance that arose seemed well
worth the effort and added a subtle patina to one's daily life —
or so I thought. Instant coffee, of course, was despised and none
was allowed in the house. You cannot get freshly roasted beans
on an island in winter time, short of growing them yourself —
and this may yet be attempted in the foreseeable future — so
what do you do when you are faced with the certainty of being
cut off from the mainland? You do a volte-face and get in a good
stock of instant granules by the one and a half pound tin. It is
served in thick brown earthenware mugs and, made with island
spring water, it really is quite delicious.

Bread is another case in point. Nowadays we bake our own as
a matter of course, but in those first early days stores and baking
were out of the question and the only food we had was what Babs
managed to bring with her. A loaf of bread, therefore, was
something to be prized and cosseted. It may not make the
Guinness Book of Records but, when alone on the island, I did
stretch out one loaf to last three and a half weeks. Certainly it
grew a mould at intervals, but the answer to this was simple;

you scraped the mould off and put the loaf in the Aga to freshen it. I had one rough rule of thumb: mould on meat, fish or fowl was a 'BAD THING' and out went the offending items to the ever-eager gulls. Mould on grain subjects such as bread came into the category, according to my reckoning, of penicillin, and therefore, in moderation, should have no deleterious effect. Question? How can gulls survive on putrefying flesh that would poison humans and pets? Answer: I do not know. Question? How did I survive this crude distinction? Answer: I do not know, but some nineteen years later I am writing this!

The foregoing will, I hope, answer in part, those who ask 'How did you make out in those primitive conditions after the ease and comfort of civilized suburban life?' The simple fact is that you have to adapt. Not everyone can do so and only those who can should try island life. Babs and I are of the vintage that is supposedly set in its ways. If we were we would have taken the first boat back to the mainland. On the other hand we have had day visitors, half our age, who ask rather fussily 'where is the separate "Ladies" and "Gents"?' As this is our home and not a railway station, I say as pleasantly as I can: 'Where yours is in your home'. If they only realized how lucky they were that we could offer them any such facilities at all! Having a lavatory that worked and having enough water to flush it was one of the major luxuries of life that we aspired to but did not always attain, in those early days. 'Water, water everywhere, nor any drop to drink,' was not only our theme song but, as a variation on a theme, we could have added 'nor any drop to flush'. Nowadays we have, we think, reached the height of sophistication in pumping sea-water to perform this vital service. How this came about must wait to be told later in our island saga.

However, at this time we felt that things were beginning to look up. The generator started after a fashion, the Aga was going merrily, we had a water supply, and we had beds to sleep in. What more could we ask? Well we could ask how we were to cope with the daffodils that were peeping up in all directions. Before doing anything about them we were delighted to find a boiler in the outhouse under the bathroom. To our great joy we

managed to get this going and were able to luxuriate in hot
baths; wrapped in hot towels from the tank in the airing
cupboard we felt that we had reached the very pinnacle of
gracious living.

Now that our creature comforts were taken care of, we
concentrated on our more immediate plans. Anne volunteered
to help sort out the books and first there was much shuntings of
bookcases. The biggest was one that our brother, Tom, had
made from an enormous kitchen dresser, when he was a young
man. This was about 8 feet tall and 8 feet wide, and after a
perilous journey across the sea in an open boat, was now housed
in our ex-barn/transit camp adjoining Jetty Cottage. This
became the home for many of the classics. Also in this huge
room were some built-in bookshelves and these stored a
miscellany of our guide books, maps, foreign dictionaries,
primers and the like. Up in the house Anne tried valiantly to
sort according to categories and size, an almost impossible task
as they ranged from huge bound copies of *The Illustrated London
News, circa* 1879, to small pocket editions. Our tastes were
catholic to say the least, and over the years we had amassed a
sizeable collection on varying subjects covering history, poetry,
music, art, archaeology, biography, philosophy, belles lettres,
mountaineering, wildlife, the theatre, travel, astronomy,
cricket, cookery, pottery, photography, gardening, assorted
crafts, to name a few, as well as several sets of encyclopaedia.
Some subjects needed several shelves apiece. Anne burst out
laughing when she came to the section on 'Retirement and How
to Enjoy It'. She wondered if we ourselves had written them.
She was not alone in this opinion. Our mother, who had a
wonderful facility for summing up a situation or expressing an
opinion in a succinct phrase, had once said, when I proudly
showed her my latest book acquisition: 'All the books you buy,
dear, you could write yourself.' I would agree with her over the
books on retirement, and now that Babs has joined me we could
certainly tell the world 'How to Enjoy Retirement', although I
must admit our way would not be to everyone's taste.

Brian elected to carry on with chipping the channel through

the rocks to the jetty — the first of my 'friends' to whom I thankfully relinquished this task. Our major concern was to sow as much as possible in the marvellously fertile soil and harvest the daffodils which were now appearing in different parts of the island. With great excitement we picked our very first bunches and as we gathered them we remembered how expensive they were in the towns and cities at this time of the year, and what a breath of spring they brought in our cold winters high up on Epsom Downs in Surrey. We wanted as many as possible, for Babs only had two days' holiday for her half-term and it would not be very long before Wren would be coming to fetch her. Suddenly we espied him rowing across from Hannafore, for the sea was coming in fast from the east and it was not possible for any boats to leave the harbour. Valerie was with him, and we admired her for this, for it was no weather, sea-wise, just for an outing. In spite of what must have been a bumpy trip for Valerie, with great patience she showed us how to bunch daffodils the professional way, for her parents had a large farm and she had grown up with dealing with the early daffodils for which Cornwall is famous; so we were very glad of her expertise.

While this was in progress Wren joined Brian at chipping away at the channel to the jetty. Then to celebrate our very first daffodils we had a lunch of wine, ham salad and chips followed by fruit salad and cream, served with a flourish in the pottery soup bowls I had thrown on the wheel at Epsom School of Art. These were glazed oatmeal and white; they had ear-like lugs but they were not quite uniform in size. However, they were my very first set of thrown pieces and An O'Neill, my pottery teacher, kindly said that this distinguished them from mass-produced factory ware. She fostered them by firing them especially so that we could take them to the island as a memento of my time at the Art School. Later, a sculptor who stayed with us for a while on the island and helped me with pottery, instructed me in the making of moulds and produced a master-mould of one of the soup bowls so that these works of art should not be lost to posterity.

Some have remarked on the clarity with which these meals of

so long ago are recalled in fine detail. The truth is that it was a miracle that we ate at all, as we had no stores, no produce and no deep freeze. Each meal, then, was a triumph to be remembered and lovingly recalled. To be self-sufficient in food is essential if one is to survive on an island. Now that Babs is here all the time it is even more important. It is one of our more enjoyable projects to produce gourmet meals from very simple ingredients, and we have become expert in the use of left-overs. Nothing is ever wasted and if any food exceeds its life expectancy one of the cats is summoned to act as 'taster'. When I wintered here alone I reckoned that I could go for three months without duplicating the menu and only cooking from scratch once a week. Although we now have a deep freeze that can be run from our electrical supply (always supposing that the generator does not go on strike), we still employ these prudent techniques, ones that could be used just as well on the mainland, with much saving in time and money, with the added bonus of eating tasty, unadulterated food.

Alas! it was soon time for Wren to take Babs back from her short break. It was almost dark when the three of them, plus the precious daffodils, rowed off in the fibreglass dinghy. Babs, for some reason was sitting aloft the trolley which would be needed to haul the boat up over the rocks at Hannafore. Soon they were swallowed up in the darkness, and nothing could be heard but the roar of the sea. I had given Babs a lamp to signal when they were safely across for there was a strong tide running from the east and I was concerned for their safety in that tiny craft — a mere eight feet in length. I was greatly relieved, therefore, after some twenty minutes, to see a tiny light winking at us from the mainland. Later Babs told me that the journey had been very bouncy as the freshening sea smacked the dinghy broadside on. Perched aloft on the trolley she found herself bounced up and down, sometimes riding high in the air, and the next moment coming hard down on the iron bars. It must have been frightening to be tossed high above a tiny dinghy in pitch darkness, but seemingly she was quite unperturbed by the danger. The after effects were all that concerned her, for she was bruised black and blue, and she found it extremely painful to sit down for several days.

Brian and Anne were to be with me for a few more days so we carried on with what seemed the more important tasks, sowing vegetables seeds and onion sets, sorting out the books and getting the furniture in some sort of order. Books and their housing, although they seemed to dominate my thoughts, were only one of many problems. For almost the first time in my life I began to sleep badly. Sleep had never been a problem, except when we were enduring the anguish of wondering if the island would ever be ours. Although lacking in other skills I was lucky enough to possess the ability to sleep at will. A flick of the finger and I could be out like a light, anywhere, anytime, and could awaken to order in as little as two minutes if necessary. These catnaps would recharge the batteries until the small hours, so that five hours per night were sufficient to give long periods out of the twenty-four hours for the highly interesting and compulsive activities that life has to offer. This ability to be on nodding terms with another world, so to speak, sometimes has its disadvantages. Once when I was young I was cycling along country lanes with my schoolgirl friend, Tommy. She turned to speak to me and was horrified to see that I was fast asleep and was heading straight for a hedge. Sadly this facility for instant deep and refreshing sleep had now forsaken me. Every hour or so I would awaken, my mind buzzing with all the things to do, and new schemes chasing each other around my head. While I slept intermittently I dreamed whole films, in colour, with complicated plots and exciting and dramatic endings, and complete symphonies played by a full orchestra, in stereo. They were all completely imaginary — just figments of a fevered brain. The only thing that got me off to sleep again, when I did awaken, was the compulsion to see the end of the film with its denouement, or to make sure that I was there for the grande finale of the last movement of the symphony.

This would never do. The precious energy essential for these early pioneering days was being drained away. For pioneering it certainly was. We had taken on a whole island complete with

daffodil farm and market garden, a house and outhouses, two
cottages in a sad state of disrepair, farm buildings and
machinery, an orchard, a generator, a water-pump in the cliff,
three boats, a boathouse, three outboard engines, and we knew
precious little about running any of them. On top of this we
planned to superimpose our own activities. High on the list was
a pottery. A building abutting the generator room had been
earmarked for this. The Jetty Cottage outhouse was to be
converted into a darkroom for the all-important photography.
Somewhere had to be found for Babs's stone-cutting and
polishing equipment. Then we planned to keep hens, goats,
start a vineyard and practise other crafts for which we never had
the time; on the list were wood carving, copper enamelling,
marquetry, woodwork, leatherwork and painting. What we
had not foreseen was that the heady excitement of actually living
on an island and seeing the vast potential would spark off fresh
ideas daily. It was an though an invisible electrical current
galvanized our brains. Neither had we the wit to realize that
what we planned would require an army of technicians, farm
labourers, builders and the like, when our entire labour force
totalled one resident lady pensioner, and weekends only —
wind, weather and tide permitting — Babs, Wren and two
schoolboys. The most important factor that we seemed
incapable of facing up to was, that under these primitive
conditions, or at least conditions lacking in the modern
amenities to which we were accustomed, actual day-to-day
living would consume so much time and energy. We have often
wondered how, on that radio programme *Desert Island Discs*, the
castaways had the strength left to put on or listen to their eight
records, let alone the time to browse through Shakespeare, the
Bible and the tome of their choice. For us, in those early days,
surviving was a full-time occupation — and often still is.

No wonder then, sleep was fitful and feverish. Inexplicably,
with our usual proclivity for brushing aside major problems,
trivialities were the most troublesome. So often it was the worry
of items forgotten or mislaid that jolted one into wakefulness.
One instance of this forgetfulness was a chicken that Babs had

kept in the fridge in the cottage on the mainland, intending to bring it over to the island at the first opportunity, knowing how short of food of any kind we were. This she did. We put it in the lounge in the sunshine to make sure that it would be thoroughly thawed — then promptly forgot about it. About a week after she returned to the mainland I came across it, looking rather sad. However, I popped it into the Aga, which was now burning beautifully. It seemed to recover in this new environment. Greatly daring we ate it. It tasted delicious. Once again we lived to tell the tale that our friends of our more fastidious days would have found hard to believe.

This sleeplessness, however, left me exhausted and quite unfit for our strenuous physical life, until I hit on the idea, like others before me, of having a pencil, paper and torch by my bedside. This did the trick for although I still awakened frequently, when once I had jotted down the brilliant idea or location of lost articles, sleep came again instantly.

All too soon it was time for the Rainforths to leave. I picked bunches of daffodils for them to distribute among our many friends back in Surrey, including the O'Neills from the Art School and of course themselves. Wren brought Babs back for the weekend, loaded up the *Islander* with all the luggage, then made the startling suggestion that I might like to accompany them to the mainland and he would bring me back. This I had no wish to do at all. As far as I was concerned the island was my life from now on, and the mainland held no attractions for me whatever. It is a feeling that persists to this day, and I only go when absolutely necessary for visits to the hairdresser, dentist, etc. and an annual foray for stores. A visit for pleasure just does not enter into the scheme of things. We have everything we want here: books, music, TV, innumerable hobbies, the market garden and daffodils, and above all the ever-changing sea and the beauty of the island itself, *and* we have no traffic, no clanging of the telephone, no supermarkets and no neighbour trouble. I was, therefore, horrified at Wren's suggestion and was adamant that I would make my farewells here. Wren, however, was very persuasive and cajoled me into going by promising that he would show me how to run the *Islander* on the way over, and I could bring it back. So after a pleasant instructional trip it was goodbye to the Rainforths and hello to Zena who came over to the cottage and made us all a cup of tea. Zena was one of the first of the Cornish friends we had made during our enforced six weeks' stay on the mainland until we made our final move over to the island. She had identified herself so much with our island project that it was a joy to see her again.

I then had the great thrill of steering the *Islander* all the way back. 'A perfect landing!' announced Wren as I beached her with a satisfying scrunch. Now, as a bonus, I was allowed to take part in a more horrendous operation of working the caterpillar tractor. 'Allowed' was hardly the word for I had no desire whatever to be a tractor driver. But Wren is not only very persuasive, he enjoys passing on his skills to others who may benefit from their use. As I have found, often to my cost, that 'Yes' slips more easily off the tongue than 'No', I now found myself gingerly mounting this fearsome monster.

The reason for using it was exciting enough. A few days previously we had espied on the east side of the main beach one round and two hexagonal hand-hewn pieces of granite or stone, each about a yard in diameter and several inches thick. They had been exposed by an exceptionally big spring tide. As far as Wren knew — and he had known the island all his life — they had never been seen before. How long they had been buried in the sand and what exactly they were we still do not know. It was a most exciting find, however, for the extraordinary thing was that one of them was similar to those on the chapel site on top of the hill. According to the records the chapel, which no longer exists except for a few remaining stones, was built in 1139. The two hexagonal stones were of granite and matched those of a granite structure sited by the house. This is of unknown origin. We were told by the Whitehouses that it was the font from the chapel; although there is no proof of this there is obviously some connection between this, the remains on the chapel site and now these stones found, inexplicably, high up on the beach. If they were not to be buried again by another spring tide, perhaps for centuries, it was essential to move them soon.

That this important, and to my mind, dangerous operation was to be performed there and then by just Wren and me seemed utterly preposterous, for it was seemingly impossible to budge them one inch. Wren now proceeded to demonstrate his skill at levering. First he managed to prise one up an inch or two with a plank. My job was to push another plank into the gap thus made. Wren then raised the stone a few more inches and I pushed another plank in. So this prising, levering and pushing went on until these three most unwieldy and heavy objects were slowly and carefully lifted and manoeuvred on to the truck. This was now harnessed to the tractor where I reigned in unmitigated terror. Scarcely recovered from my menial but nevertheless nerve-racking task of plank pushing, I was now commanded to pull various levers, and 'have a go'. The monster jolted into life beneath me and amid much screeching from below, and yells from Wren, above the roar of the engine, we were away, a ten-foot perpendicular drop to the beach below, an unpleasantly close few inches to my left, luckily avoided. As we reached the top of the path Babs came running out of the house to see what all the racket was about, and I do not suppose my terror-stricken face allayed her fears. At last, to my intense relief, our precious burden was deposited by the bank at the side of the house, and there these relics remain awaiting some expert to identify them.

Thus, in the space of an hour or so, I had not only made an unexpected trip to the mainland, but had learned how to handle an eighteen-foot diesel motor-boat, driven a tractor, learned a little about the art of levering and had helped rescue these important finds and bring them to a place of safety. With hindsight I realized, of course, that Wren had planned all of these happenings from the beginning.

The ─── **DAFFODIL FARMERS'** *Tale*

Now that the Rainforths had departed, Babs and I planned our time until Sunday when Wren would bring Ruth over to the island and take Babs back to the mainland. First we decided that we must have a 'sort out'. Not all is glamour or even sheer hard work on an island, although there is always plenty of the latter. Some of it is merely fretful, just as it is on the mainland. Precious hours of her stay were spent in 'sorting out'. This seems endemic to our island life, for even to this day this occupation dominates our lives as much as the weather does. The Queen may be dogged by red despatch boxes, but we are dogged by looking for lost items. We look at each other through clenched teeth and mutter, 'We will have to have a "sort out" ', but how time-consuming it is! Seemingly possessions are like weeds — many of them are the right things in the wrong places, at least they are for us. We have a house, a couple of cottages, sheds, outhouses and a generator room to confuse us. We wonder what it must be like to live in a castle or palace with dozens of rooms to search through for lost items. I am also puzzled by the fact that an inert object like a ball-point pen seems to have a life of its own. Although we buy them by the dozen they will all elude us and find some secret hiding place known only to themselves. I am sure that if this island is excavated in a thousand years time some archaeologist will mark on his map: 'Possible site of early ball-point pen factory?'

With spring upon us, however, sowing and planting seemed more important than dealing with inanimate objects. With much enthusiasm we sowed sweet peas, tomatoes, sweet corn, runner beans and melons, and made cuttings of carnations. All of these were started in an unheated greenhouse, so convinced were we that spring came very early indeed to the island, judging by the daffodils that were now coming up almost everywhere.

The main daffodil fields are between the house and the main beach. They slope down from the woods almost to the cliff edge, separated from this only by the path to the beach. They are divided by colourful hedges of pink escallonia and purple veronica and are fenced off from the path by ash palings. These fences were obviously intended to act as wind-breaks, for these fields are exposed to the full force of gales from a northerly or an easterly direction. Some of the fences hung around in a drunken fashion and gave us some idea of the strength of the winds.

When we explored the top of the island we found more daffodil fields exposed to the south and south-west, and the fences here, although protected by impenetrable brambles, were in an even worse state of repair. It looked as though they had been laid waste by a hurricane. This, in fact, is exactly what had happened, and we found, in the course of time, that winds of storm force ten and even hurricane force twelve have ravaged them from time to time.

Fencing then would be a major problem, and we began to realize that there was more to cultivating daffodils than picking pretty bunches when the rest of the country was under snow and ice. In view of the havoc that the winds could cause we were puzzled that along the path from the house to the beach some of the fencing had been replaced by embryo privet hedges. As these were spindly little cuttings of some twelve inches high we wondered what protection they would give to the daffodils and what advantages they had over fences. Although we did not appreciate it then, the planting of the privet was a wise alternative to fencing. In less than seven years we had a row of fine thick hedges and now they are so high that it takes a tall person on a step-ladder to trim them. In fact they look as though they have been there since the days of Elizabeth I. This has given rise to a fancy of mine that we might construct a maze, although it is a matter of doubt if we would ever have the time to plant and tend it. Many were the times, over the next few winters, when I wished that the previous owners had planted those cuttings earlier in the life of the island as a daffodil farm, for every time there was a gale, down would come some fences. From the very beginning of our life here people have said: 'How I envy you living on an island!' Perched on a step-ladder dragged up to the top of the island in the teeth of a gale, banging in posts with a sledge-hammer, the rain streaming down the neck of my oilskins and the ladder swaying precariously in the wind, I have often wondered if they know what island life is really like. It is a continual battle with the elements, and charging around with a step-ladder and a sledge-hammer in a full gale with icy rain slashing against your face is only one of the many hazards met with in this 'idyllic' life, as we were to find out. Nevertheless, the sense of achievement in overcoming the problems and challenges far outweighs the feelings of despair that threaten to engulf us as some new crisis rears its head.

Although not physically demanding, the next problem we faced was a knotty one. Of the fifteen varieties, which were which? Although in our ignorance we thought that all daffodils were the same — yellow — we could now see that each field was quite different. Some were indeed yellow with large trumpets, others were smaller and had red centres; others again were white with yellow centres. Anyway, we decided, it did not really matter for there were not enough in bloom in any one field to fill a box. At Epsom Downs we had been introduced by phone to Mr Myers, the wholesaler at Covent Garden to whom the Whitehouses sent their daffodils. A friend of ours happened to be a family friend of the Myers and so a useful contact was made. Mr Myers had offered to give us any advice that we might need. We did not think that we needed it just yet. The Whitehouses had left behind an assortment of boxes, tissue paper, brown paper, string and other impedimenta to do with the marketing of daffodils. We now knew from Valerie how to bunch them professionally, so on the Sunday, before Babs returned to the mainland, with loving care we bunched up the choicest blooms of all the different varieties that were then in flower, and packed them artistically and with much care in one of the boxes. They looked really beautiful and we closed the lid, sealed and addressed it with a certain amount of reluctance and a great deal of pride. There were some bunches over, so Babs took some back with her to distribute to our friends in Looe and to take to school. At the cottage Babs made out the invoice and securely tied the box for its journey by train to Covent Garden; took it by car to the station, and, much as a fond mother might wave her young son off to his first prep school, saw it safely ensconced in solitary state among the thousands of boxes already on their journey from the Isles of Scilly via Penzance to London in the 'Flower Special'.

Zena and Charles took the remainder and sold them locally at the current rate of 1s. 8d. per bunch, much to Babs's surprise but delight. We had marketed our very first daffodils — we were now established daffodil farmers! We came down to earth with a bump when we received a letter from Mr Myers. It was very friendly and polite but he would like to point out that each box should contain one variety of daffodil only — a mixed box would not do for marketing wholesale.

This posed quite a problem. We knew each field grew a different variety and we had inherited a load of impressive looking labels printed with the name 'ST GEORGE'S ISLAND' in large capitals followed by VARIETY: QUANTITY: with appropriate spaces left for entering the details, and addressed to MYERS & CO., COVENT GARDEN, LONDON. We now had to resolve the problem as to which label applied to which variety. How does one distinguish 'Magnificence', 'Scilly White', 'Unsurpassable', 'Fortune', 'Mount Hood', 'Aranjuez', 'Cragford', 'Yellow Cheerfulness', 'Beersheba', 'St Agnes', 'Scarlet Gem', 'Sempre Avanti' (so evocative of musical evenings) and 'King Alfred'? The following weekend Babs and I went down to Jetty Cottage, which at that time was a more or less derelict building; we picked our way over joists that exposed the bare earth beneath, to a room floored by concrete. This had obviously been used as a packing station and an adjoining room as the office. Here among the papers we found a list of daffodils with the prices fetched against each kind. We decided to name the daffodils, as each field in turn became ready for picking, in the order in which the list was written, and we would label them accordingly. Surprisingly enough this worked, for during the whole time we sent them to Covent Garden we never had our labelling queried, although we ourselves were never sure of the difference between 'St Agnes' and 'Cragford' — they were so alike — one being a bigger version of the other; probably, we thought, an older sister. We hoped that soon we should have enough of each variety fo fill the appropriate box.

During the following week I inspected the fields. I had heard somewhere that it was the present-day method to pick and pack the daffodils when in tight bud, and it seemed to me that one field was at this stage. Ruth had resumed her de-rusting of the buoy, and she was rubbing down her 'land-mine' as if it was meant to be the most gleaming bit of metal in a war museum of torpedoes and the like. I persuaded her to leave this operation for a short time to inspect the daffodils. 'Too tight!' said Ruth, 'the necks have to bend over.' Nevertheless, thrilled that we should have enough to fill several boxes, and afraid that by the weekend they would be in full flower and past their peak for the tight bud condition required, I said: 'Let's get them over to Babs anyway. They will probably bend over later,' I added hopefully. In the end we decided to pick those that looked as though they were thinking about performing the required gymnastics; get them over to Babs, and if there were not enough to send to Covent Garden they could be sold locally.

We proceeded to launch the fibreglass dinghy with a fair amount of argument as to the best method to stop it going in circles and drifting back, high and dry, on the beach again, without getting wet ourselves. The difficulty was that it required a certain depth of water to float the dinghy in the first place. By the time we managed to clamber into the bobbing craft the combined weight of our two selves and the daffodils, and the fact that the tide was going out, set us back on dry land again. There we were — in spite of all our pushing, shoving and heaving of ourselves, pulling on the oars or trying to punt off with them — sitting in the dinghy on the beach for all the world as though we were about to have a picnic. There was obviously much more to launching a boat than we realized — Wren had made it look so easy. However, after more argument and a great deal of laughter we managed to flounder into the boat and at last got away with our precious boxes of daffodils.

The sea was calm for a change so there was no difficulty in rowing across to Hannafore. The problem was in finding the right channel through the rocks. Mr Whitehouse had told us how to line up various landmarks to find the way in; the best apparently being the sewerage channel, as this would take us right up to Hannafore beach. This involved negotiating a vast area of rocks. Soon they were looming above us in all directions, and we were lost in a labyrinth of pinnacles. In and out and around, we pushed and prodded with the oars, but as the tide receded we soon found ourselves almost high and dry and marooned. We scrambled out and tried to pull the boat higher up the gully in which we found ourselves. We pulled her as far up as we could and did our best to tie the rope round one of the rocks. Then we lifted out our precious boxes of daffodils and somehow managed to slither our way over the rocks to the shore.

Up at the cottage we waited for Babs to come home from school. She was delighted to see us and thrilled to have the daffodils. She came round to Hannafore to see us off but to our consternation the boat was not there; the tide had turned and taken it away. Panic now ensued. A kindly gentleman, Mr Curtis, came to the rescue and not only gave us a lift back to West Looe but arranged for Jack Dingle, a local boat owner, to collect the drifting boat and take us back to the island. The sea had strengthened with the incoming tide and Jack Dingle said that it was too dangerous to land us on the main beach. He therefore landed us and the dinghy safely on the eastern side of the beach and we were very grateful to him and Mr Curtis for saving the day. It was not quite the end of our disasters however. We found that the sea had taken away the wheelbarrow in which we had transported the daffodils down to the shore and the trolley for the dinghy. However, all was not lost, as the saying goes. The next day the outgoing tide gave us back both the wheelbarrow and the trolley; we were able to rescue both and by washing them with rain-water to counteract the effect of the salt sea-water, and by the diligent application of grease to the vital metal parts we were able to put them to good use again. As a further consolation Babs got the top prices for the daffodils she sent to Covent Garden and Zena the excellent price of 1s. 9d. a bunch for those she sold locally for us. We began to think that we really *were* daffodil farmers.

We were soon to realize how true this was. Daffodils began to spring up everywhere — the fields were a sea of gold. We blacked-out every conceivable room and outhouse on the island and filled them with bucket after bucket of daffodils, for the darkness necessary to keep them in bud as long as possible. Babs came at the weekend and we all three bunched and boxed, bunched and boxed. Babs took them back to the cottage on the mainland and was up until the early hours, labelling, invoicing and tying up the boxes. Then before going to school in the morning she loaded the car and delivered the boxes to the station to catch the Flower Special.

The following weekend Barry, a relative by marriage, his wife Margaret, and Dave Tank, their brother-in-law, came to help. Margaret was almost lost to sight as she staggered under the huge loads of daffodils larger than herself. Incredibly we managed to bunch and box them all and with some loss of sleep by Babs they caught the Flower Special. Relentlessly, however, the daffodils continued to spring up everywhere — the whole island seemed to be covered with them. My ribs began to ache with so much stooping and the soreness was so severe that I could not sleep, it was like a nagging toothache and the pain pierced my side every time I breathed; but I could not stop — the daffodils *had* to be gathered. I picked about 800 to 1,000 each session with little time between for a snack. We then had to load them into buckets and lug these around the island so that we could find some protection of darkness for them, for the hot March sun would bring the buds out in full flower if we did not hurry. Soon the white 'Beersheba' reached their peak. This was the largest and most prolific field of all; a large and elegant white daffodil, it resembled a lily and always fetched tip-top prices at Covent Garden. Even in a glut year 'Beershebas' always held their price for they were in great demand for weddings and funerals; locally they were not so popular, as they were considered to be too funereal. As they were destined for Covent Garden and would be in transit for a long time, they had to be in the very peak of condition, that is, in tight bud, so we were under great pressure to lift them and store them in darkness. There seemed to be millions of these white daffodils in that field — it was like trying to eliminate the Milky Way. We were absolutely loaded with daffodils everywhere, for it was the very height of the season. We knew that Wren was due in two days time so we changed from picking to bunching. This was a relief for my painful side but there was still a great deal of physical lugging about of buckets, heavy with water as well as the flowers, for now the difficulty was in finding dark rooms, for the bunches took up more room than the gathered armfuls.

The day Wren was due it was brilliantly sunny, with the sea a Mediterranean blue — even in London the temperature was seventy-five degrees, very high for March. The sea, however, was making up and white horses began to appear. The wind was freshening all the time from the dreaded easterly direction. Nevertheless we had to start the long job of boxing the bunches to be ready should Wren come. In the early evening Babs and Wren appeared on the beach at Hannafore. They signalled across — it was too rough. Despondently we unpacked the boxes and hastily made wire frames to fit the baths in the cottages to support the precious bunches, for already some of the buds were beginning to open and must not be crushed. We also had another problem. All the seeds which Babs and I had sown so enthusiastically had now germinated and should be pricked out, and, in the hot greenhouse temperature, needed watering and constant attention. No wonder a book on horticulture had said that it was not possible to grow daffodils commercially and run a smallholding efficiently, for both required undivided attention at the same time.

The next day it was still sunny and warm but with an easterly gale lashing in. If Wren were to come that night it would have to be about 11 p.m., at low tide, when there would be the chance of a temporary lull. At our regular time for signalling Babs appeared at Hannafore — apparently he was going to try. That would mean using his own dinghy from Hannafore as no boat could leave the harbour. Ruth and I then raced from cottage to cottage and the outhouses, gathering up buckets of daffodils, and we then proceeded to box them again. We had to hurry, so there was no time to drain the bunches thoroughly and they had to be packed with care. In all there were twenty-two large boxes and four smaller ones and each was so heavy it was difficult to manhandle them. We were still desperately tying up the boxes when we espied lights wavering down over the rocks at Hannafore. The lights congregated on the rocks and for a long time there was no visible movement and utter silence except for the howling of the wind. We were frantically tying up the last of the boxes when we heard the sound of the tractor coming up the path. As we helped load the boxes on to the truck, Wren told us that Babs, his wife Valerie, and Zena and her son Charles were all over at Hannafore. It had been a treacherous climb down over the slippery rocks. He had informed the coastguard in case he found himself in difficulties because it was a hazardous expedition, even for Wren; there was an easterly gale blowing, the low tide had exposed a mass of dangerous rocks and all this had to be negotiated in pitch darkness. We flashed a signal with our Tilley lamp that he had arrived safely, then made our way back down the path. It was no easy matter for Wren to drive the tractor for the trees overhead intensified the darkness and our lamp did little to help. We managed to move our heavy metal boat to the water's edge for this was needed to take the bulk of the boxes. We flashed again that Wren was about to start on this quite perilous journey. He then set off standing up in the boat, piled high with boxes and, pushing from the shore with an oar, he glided off into the night looking for all the world like a gondolier.

Fraught with anxiety we sheltered in the boathouse.

Suddenly the Tilley lamp gave out and the intense blackness of the night that now enveloped us only added to the nervous tension. After a long interval we at last heard the welcome scrunch of the boat on the shingle as Wren emerged once more out of the gloom. We now had to manhandle the metal boat up the beach and this was no easy matter, even for the three of us, on the upward slope from dead low tide. Wren now had to row back in his own boat.

As far as Ruth and I were concerned this was the end of the operation, but for the others it was just beginning. All the heavy boxes and Wren's boat had to be hauled up the seaweed-strewn rocks. Added to this Valerie had a bad back, and Zena was not allowed to lift anything, so she was the very necessary lamplighter-in-chief and cheer-leader. One box fell in a pool and the precious contents of Beersheba were drenched with sea-water. In spite of this, we were relieved to find later that they had come to no harm and, with the rest of the consignment, fetched the top price. Finally all the boxes were hauled up, but the boat was another matter, and in the end Wren carried it up on his back. About 1.45 a.m. they signalled that the car was loaded with the first consignment and, the perils over, we broke off all communication.

With all the weaving of lamps up and down the rocks and the shore on either side of the channel it must have appeared to any onlookers who were around in the small hours of the morning that a big smuggling operation was taking place, or that villains were up to some nefarious deeds. For what right-minded citizens would choose dead of night around 2 a.m. in an easterly gale for an innocent expedition? We were thankful Wren had taken the precaution of informing the coastguard. Transport was not only one-way. Babs had sent over a parcel of a daily paper, bread and some biscuits. Back at the house about 2.30 a.m. we made hot chocolate and fell on the biscuits, for we were frozen stiff and had scarcely eaten anything but snacks for days.

We knew that Babs would not be quite so fortunate for she now had the task of invoicing and tying up the boxes in pairs, ready for transporting by car in the morning to take them to the station to catch the Flower Special. As a consequence she did not get to bed until nearly 4 a.m. and was up at 6.30 a.m. as she would have to make at least two journeys to ferry them before going to school. Aware that something like that would be happening I felt I was in honour bound to get up early too, so I forced myself out of bed and climbed to the fields at the top of the island to pick the St Agnes — or were they Cragford? Toby always accompanied me on all these expeditions and sat at the end of each row as I picked. It was surprising what a comfort and encouragement this was, but I do not think it was any surprise to Toby — he knew — that was why he was there. Ruth and I, both very much under the weather, did not meet up for some time, leaving notes for each other to log our movements, but we did get together for a late lunch of boiled eggs. This cheered us up enormously, especially as I was able to report finding a patch of cultivated violets beyond the carnations, both of which we were to discover grow exceptionally well here. That afternoon we were able to put out several boxes of runner beans, lettuce and sweet corn in the capacious Dutch lights which we had found at the back of the tractor shed. The beautiful Scarlet Gem daffodils were coming into bloom — it was a lovely sunny day and, although the east wind was cold, all seemed right with the world.

The daffodils would soon be coming to an end. The difficulty now was to have some for the lucrative Easter market. With our early season this is not always possible. In fact the economics of daffodil growing is a chancy business, as is all farming. If it were a sparse year the prices would be high but there were not enough to send to market to get a good income. On the other hand in a glut year prices slumped and one slaved away night and day to harvest and market them for very little income. In fact we heard on the radio, in one glut year, when the Scillies sent huge quantities, they were burning them at Covent Garden. Unlike other goods where the manufacturer fixes his prices based on cost, with flowers Covent Garden fixes the price, based presumably on the demand. It is essential therefore to catch the market at its peak, for the overheads of labour, packaging, transport and handling fees are constant whatever the return. With the added cost and difficulties of transport over the sea, daffodil harvesting and marketing is a time of much hard work and anxiety. We had yet to face the actual cultivation of daffodils and the techniques involved. Our life as daffodil farmers had only just begun.

Before this there were other major matters to be considered. The most important was what to do about the derelict cottages. Soon, too, Ruth would be leaving and two potter boys from Epsom School of Art, as arranged by Dennis O'Neill, Head of the Department of Pottery, would be coming to help with my pottery.

The
NEWCOMERS'
Tale

However, before we had formulated any precise plans about restoring the cottages there were several unexpected happenings. Two of them took me very much by surprise.

One evening I went down the path to the main beach to await a signal from Babs. I was alone and as I peered into the darkness to look for a winking light I suddenly felt something press against my leg. Although easily frightened, for some unknown reason I felt no fear. I put my hand down and felt a warm furry body and, when I switched on the torch, looking up at me was the appealing face of a beautiful tabby cat; our island cat had revealed herself at last! She stayed for a while nestling in my arms — then as suddenly as she had appeared she was gone.

Thereafter, whenever I walked alone she would appear for a while and then disappear, just like the Cheshire cat. Toby, who must have sensed what was going on, was now always on the look-out. One day he found her and chased her to her cliff-top home, and I was afraid that one day he would go headlong to the rocks below. But he never chased her again, and I think it was just to find out and show me where she lived, for having made his mark he seemed satisfied. They must have come to some understanding for as I worked in the fields Toby stood guard at one end of the row while she sat at the other, both ostensibly ignoring each other. One day she appeared at the kitchen window appealing to come in. As she diffidently did so I wondered how Toby would take it. Apart from their both wanting a great deal of affection from me, this historic moment passed well enough. Toby, however, would not eat his meals for several days, and would only accept the choicest hand-fed tit-bits. I felt torn between divided loyalties, but I need not have worried. Gradually Cleo, as Babs and I decided to call her, won Toby round. She took up residence in the kitchen, and in her gentle almost timid way made up to Toby. He, as always, the perfect gentleman, responded by letting her through doors first (as he always did for us), and eventually allowed her to share his meals. She would rub up against him affectionately, and it was a relationship that was to last for the rest of his life. We felt we were fortunate to have him with us still, for he had been affected by a heart condition long before we came to the island, and soon he would be fourteen years old.

The second surprise was sprung on me by Babs. She bought a goat! Although we had considered keeping goats at some time in the future, it was a subject about which we knew nothing and we reckoned it needed some study before we embarked on becoming goatherds.

It was not, however, a premeditated purchase — more an impulse buy. It happened that Babs was staying for the weekend with a friend of hers, Ann Coon. The house overlooked the backyard of a pet shop that existed in Looe at the time, but is no longer there. In this yard was a small white kid and the whole weekend it cried and cried. This was too much for Babs. First thing on Monday morning she went in and bought it. 'It' was a 'she', a white pedigree Saanen kid and she cost £4. The problem was how to get her over to the island. The pet shop agreed to keep her until the following weekend when Fred Woodley, who was doing some ferrying for us at the time, could bring her over in the *Islander*. The first I saw of her was when she gracefully leapt ashore through the *Islander's* lifebelt. She was very pretty and had friendly, smiling hazel eyes. We immediately named her Frederica, after Fred. As she had not been polled she had budding horns which later were to cause us problems, which in time because insuperable, as she became adult. Meantime she happily took up residence with us, and sleeping quarters were made up for her in the back of the tractor shed, with a bountiful supply of hay. Later we moved her to the outhouses of Smugglers' Cottage where she could have the freedom of the lawns there. Cleo did not know what to make of this new arrival, and she really looked as though she was surveying her with arms akimbo. Toby, having spent all his life until recently on the mainland, seemed to accept her quite readily, as did Cleo when once she had got over the initial shock of coming face to face with this (to her) strange-looking four-footed creature.

Meantime our population was increasing, albeit temporarily in the case of the two-legged variety. With the advent of our first summer of 1965 many friends came to help us, and we were not only a hive of industry but we actually acquired a hive of bees. We had long decided that we must have bees ever since a 'Leisure Exhibition' that Babs had organized at her school in Surrey, at which the local Bee Society had exhibited. We had since read books on the subject and could not wait to populate our island with its own self-contained civilization and factory for producing honey. Barry, who was the brother-in-law of our nephew Doug, was a bee-keeper who had at that time some forty hives, although he possesses many more now. He volunteered to set us up with a hive of bees. This he very generously did, and ever since, give or take the odd disaster that can overtake even experienced bee-keepers, we have kept bees. Some experts have told us categorically that there is not enough nectar on the island to support a hive, but every year, if the bees have not been ousted by wasps or suffered some other set-back, we have at least twenty-five to thirty-five pounds of honey and twice that amount when we have had two hives. This, our first hive, was set up in the orchard as here it would be protected by surrounding trees and hedges from the onslaught of gales.

All was not honey however, as the saying goes. As the resident sister it was decided that I should be in charge, so I was duly kitted out with veil and protective clothing. Barry visited us several times that summer to look after the bees' welfare and to give me instructions. I found it all completely fascinating and managed into the bargain to take some close-up photographs of the bees, including the Queen Bee. All went well until the time Barry came without his veil; he could not very well bring it for he swam over from Hannafore in his wet suit, catching some fish for us on the way. I lent him my veil and waited on the path outside the orchard. Barry inspected the bees, then came towards me with a section of the hive to show me something, and as he did so the bees, who must have been in an angry mood, for some reason decided to come too — in force. They then made a bee-line for me. It was like being attacked by a Lilliputian tribe of Red Indians with poisoned arrows. Barry yelled that he could not come to help or the rest would come with him. I yelled too, but somehow managed to get most of them out of my hair and made off as best I could. In all there were some thirteen stings on my face and around my eyes and it was of course very painful and swollen. That night I had palpitations. Luckily, due to my swollen eyes, I could not read the bee book to find out how to deal with the stings. It was as well, for the next day I learned that they can cause heart attacks, comas and even prove fatal.

There is no knowing what the outcome would have been if my imagination had got to work as well. However, I was so thankful that I had survived that I faced the prospect of having two teeth out that day with slightly more equanimity than might otherwise have been the case. Nevertheless, for some days I did feel that living our island life was proving more perilous perhaps than the dangers of the Second World War.

Next the bees swarmed and took up their abode in the chimney of Smugglers' Cottage. An and Dennis O'Neill, who were in charge of the Pottery Department at Epsom Art School, where I had been learning prior to our move here, were camping on the island, together with Peter Steele, another expert potter, and his family. They had all offered to come and help us with our pioneering. An and Dennis had kept bees at one time so An gallantly offered to shin up the Smugglers' roof and chimney and try to dislodge them. It was very brave of her for she, too, had been badly stung during their bee-keeping days. With An aloft and smoke from the fireplace below, eventually the chimney was cleared.

However, we came to realize that bee-keeping is not the serene occupation it may seem to those with an urban background, for we have met many other hazards on the way.

Our delectable pots of honey are, we feel, hard won, but bee-keeping is a craft that goes back to times immemorial, and it seemed a natural one to pursue in the way of life we had chosen here. We are prejudiced of course, but we do think that the flavour and quality of our honey is special, for the blossoms from which the bees draw their nectar are uncontaminated by any poisonous sprays or fumes. Even the syrup with which we feed them is made from our delicious spring water. As well as supplying us with honey the bees, of course, pollinate our fruit, flowers and vegetables, so they are of inestimable value to us and well worth the hazards. Nevertheless, when Babs retired I was happy to hand over to her the reins of Queen Bee, and when I do stand on the sidelines I make sure that I am wearing protective clothing, and then I can listen to Tennyson's 'murmuring of innumerable bees' with pleasure.

Not long after Frederica's arrival it was Toby's fourteenth birthday and, as it was during the school summer holidays, we had many friends staying with us. There were about twenty altogether including a number of children. It was decided to have a party for him on the lawn and many were the secret preparations that went on among the children. A friend of Zena's, Shirley Butlin-Jones, daughter of Billy Butlin, was holidaying on the island with her young son, William, and he had certainly inherited the family flair for showmanship. With great enthusiasm and talent he spent days beforehand organizing various forms of entertainment, including a play; this latter, unfortunately had to be abandoned as *all* the children wanted to play the leading part. Nevertheless the day promised to be a gala occasion, as indeed it was.

Cleo was the first with her greetings; first thing in the morning she rolled on the mat in front of Toby and then kissed him on the nose. Next the St George's flag was hoisted as it always is, whenever the weather makes it possible, for anniversaries, including, of course, St George's Day. Later came the tea party; tables were placed end to end on the lawn and covered with tablecloths. Janet Ayrton, who was training for Domestic Science, as it was then called, baked a gorgeous cake and the table was loaded with other goodies. Carrots and ginger-nuts, being Toby's favourites, were among the fare offered as well as cakes and jellies as they perhaps might be more generally acceptable. The children now began to arrive: all were dressed in their best party clothes, hair neatly brushed and faces and eyes shining as they presented their gifts to Toby — tins of dog meat, a ball and more carrots and ginger-nuts. How is it, one wonders, that pets can make their preferences known? Every dog we have ever had goes mad over ginger-nuts, Toby being the first to show this preference when he was very young. As far as I can remember we had never kept any in the house, so how he got the message over I cannot say, but ever since we have had to stock up with these doggy delights. Frederica came too; a pile of her favourite pellets were set in a dish before her on the table. Cleo looked in but did not stay. Cats, at least ours, do not care for parties. They will lurk in the background, heads only appearing in the bushes at barbecues, in case there are any tit-bits going. They are, however, not naturally gregarious or convivial — although Tilly, one of our present incumbents, is an exception.

Balloons were produced, games played, entertainment performed and a good time was had by all, Toby munching away happily at his carrots and ginger-nuts and Frederica scoffing her pellets. It was a lovely sunny day and a great success. A day to be remembered with gladness, but with a certain sadness, too, for it was the last birthday Toby was to have.

Soon after the birthday party our furred and feathered population began to increase. Miss Whitehouse, who had a farm outside Looe, used to row over every week when her parents left the island, to leave food for the island cat, now our gorgeous Cleo. She had asked Babs some little time ago if we would like a kitten, as a litter was due in a few weeks time. The thought of giving a new little kitten an island home appealed to us and it was arranged that Miss Whitehouse would let us know when one would be ready to leave its mother, some eight weeks after its arrival into the world.

Now came a classic example of the bush telegraph, for which surely Looe must be renowned and another instance of my penchant for being incident prone. One day during this same school summer holiday of our first year, when Babs was at last resident on her island for something longer than a brief weekend, I went ashore with the potter boys. They were two diploma course students whom Dennis and An O'Neill had arranged should stay on the island to help me set up my pottery and to assist generally. This day they were going ashore in the *Islander* to collect a load of coal and, as a last-minute decision, I hurriedly jumped into the boat with them to do some shopping.

As I stepped ashore, to my amazement, a perfect stranger came up to me and said 'Miss Whitehouse heard you were visiting the mainland; she wants to see you and is driving down into Looe shortly.' How could anyone know I was coming — I did not know myself until the last minute — and how could Miss Whitehouse, who lived several miles outside Looe, know except by precognition? Someone must have a powerful pair of binoculars and a handy telephone, I thought. But why the set-up? There seemed no reason for the island to be under constant surveillance — we were hardly the calibre to be suspected of smuggling — and with so many craft about in the bay on a summer's day, the island boat would scarcely be noticeable, let alone the identity of its occupants. And why the hot-line to Miss Whitehouse? I was soon to find out 'why' if not 'how'.

In no time at all I met up with Miss Whitehouse in the square just outside the courtyard of our cottages in West Looe. In her hand she carried a cat basket — the kitten, of course! She raised the lid and inside were three of the sweetest kittens I had ever seen. 'You can choose,' she said. There was one smaller and darker than the other two — it was minute and had a tiny appealing face. Instantly I said: 'I would like that one.' 'Wouldn't you like all three?' asked Miss Whitehouse. 'Good Heavens, No!' I almost shouted. We could not possibly feed four cats, a dog, and a goat. All those tins to transport and the worry of running short in winter gales, and other unimaginable problems — the island might become peppered with pets! 'Definitely no!' I reiterated firmly as she offered them to me again. 'Oh well!' said Miss Whitehouse, 'I shall just have to find a home for them.' She looked so worried and dejected. Suddenly she addressed passers-by in general. 'Would you like a kitten? I've *got* to find a home for these two.' This caused quite a stir but no one came forward. It was not surprising. It was not an offer to be taken up lightly, especially if your intention in being abroad was just to buy a loaf of bread, or whatever. 'They are two lovely kittens and they have nowhere to go.' She pleaded to the world at large. I suddenly felt an awful heel. How could I break up this little family group — snatch one from their midst and leave the luckless two there, and homeless to boot? 'O.K. I will have them,' I quavered. Miss Whitehouse's face lit up instantly. We repaired to *The Jolly Sailor*, handily a few yards across the square, to celebrate. I *hoped* it was a celebration, but what would Babs think? As far as she was concerned I had merely gone ashore at the last minute to do some shopping. She would not be expecting the arrival of even one kitten.

Babs came down to the beach to meet us, I stepped ashore and gingerly put the basket down. She looked questioningly at me. 'Look inside!' I said, lifting the lid gently and holding my breath. I expected a shriek at least, followed perhaps by recriminations and a lecture on taking on more responsibilities. 'How lovely!' she cried, to my intense relief, and took them to her heart instantly.

And that was how HamRam, Bessie and Joan came into our lives.

Joan was the tiny black and white tabby and was so named after Black Joan, the sister of an island smuggler of long ago. According to legends about the island, a brother and sister at one time lived here and indulged in smuggling. When the Excise Officers arrived unexpectedly, Black Joan would row out to them and divert their attention with her charms while her brother hastily hid the smuggled goods. Our kitten was well named after her; she always remained small and dainty with beautiful black and white markings. She had immense charm

—a charismatic cat if ever there was one—but she bestowed her favours sparingly. It was quite something to see a six-foot muscular man dissolve into gentleness at sight of her. 'Look!' he would cry triumphantly, 'She has *let me* pick her up.' I must confess that she was my special one, for had I not chosen her in the first place? Or maybe she had chosen me. She seemed so small and helpless, yet paradoxically, although the most feline and unattainable of the three, she had a tender heart. She made me her especial responsibility and when I was in bed with a chill or whatever, she never left me — a short necessary sortie out, a quick meal and she was back on my bed. At other times she was remote but kept a weather eye on me and honoured me sometimes by sitting on my lap. Bessie was so named because she was chubby and cuddly; she looked just like a Bessie and she was *very* fond of eating.

We had not had the kittens very long and were walking down the path one day when Toby, the gentleman, for some inexplicable reason started to chase Bessie. This was quite out of character, for he had been most solicitous towards them all. Whether he had a sudden twinge of jealousy, or if some inner voice said 'You are supposed to chase cats!' we had no way of knowing. Anyway chase her he did, all the way down to the beach and the sea. It was dark and we could not see so we called and called but there was no sign of her. Eventually we returned to the house hoping that, with Toby out of the way, she might re-appear. She did not. Supper-time was long past and still there was no sign of Bessie. We tried to console ourselves that she was merely frightened and hiding for a time, but we had actually heard her in the sea. Could kittens swim? We did not know. Sick at heart we busied ourselves washing-up in the scullery. Suddenly a face appeared at the window — Bessie! Toby made a great fuss of her and I think that he had been as worried as we were, especially as he would feel that it was not gentlemanly to chase a lady into the sea. Not that she looked wet at all. It was probably Toby who had splashed into the sea and Bessie had veered off into the rocks. In any case pets have a marvellous way of looking after themselves, but this we have never learned to accept. Many are the times we have organized search parties for missing pets, only to find them serenely awaiting our return to be let in, or in the case of cats, casually strolling up the path, having been missing for two or even three days on some secret mission.

HamRam, the third of our triplets — although it would be hard to find triplets more dissimilar in looks, size and character — was named after the most famous island smuggler of them all. In fact his name, so his descendants told us when they came on a visit, was Amram, but our HamRam had already been named so HamRam he remained. Our HamRam was no smuggler but he was a very big cat and cuddly. As he was the only boy cat he was neutered in due course. He was spoiled from the very beginning, not only by us but by Bessie, who mothered him. Later when all three became rat-catchers, he would catch only the tiddley ones and leave them for Bessie to dispose of for him.

Cleo came to inspect the kittens but, as is the enigmatic way of cats, there was no way of knowing what she thought of them. We thought we had an inkling later, because when we provided boxes in the warm kitchen for all four, the kittens chose instead to huddle together on the window-seat with Cleo in their midst. We hoped this meant that she would mother them, but this was not to be. Her ears were flattened down, a sure sign, although we did not realize it at the time as we were new to having a colony of cats, that this registered not only anti-sociability but might even be an open declaration of war, rather like a knight of old with his head and lance tilting forward to the fray. Indeed we learned later that if any of our dear, lovable cats flattened their ears thus, we would be advised to hurl ourselves out of the room to the safety of the other side of the door, collecting one of them under our arm if possible, otherwise we might find ourselves in a mêlée of flying fur and claws, and get badly scratched into the bargain. The cats meantime would suddenly resume 'normal service' of docility and sisterly and brotherly affection, while we were still staunching blood from our lacerated skins. Cleo never went beyond flattening her ears; she showed no dramatic hostility — she just did not become their surrogate mother. They, on the other hand, accepted her but were quite happy with each other. Toby was still her favourite and the one whose company she sought.

Alas! it was a friendship that was destined not to last very long. The winter following his fourteenth birthday party Toby began to weaken somewhat and became rather frail. He took to going out at night and not coming in again. He was only on the lawn—just sitting—and he would let me carry him back into the house; each time he felt lighter in weight and it became obvious that quite painlessly he was fading away. One of his specialities was singing. We did not teach him, he taught himself and he loved listening to music on the radio, joining in spontaneously when he heard any of his favourites. Two in particular he liked were 'Bless This House' and Elisabeth Schwarzkopf singing the solo in 'The Nuns' Chorus' from *Casanova* and he would always join in when these were broadcast. He would perform for visitors too, if we hummed either of these and asked him to sing. He could sing no more but he still enjoyed listening to music. One day he did not have the strength to go out nor indeed lift himself up. He lay quietly in my arms while I gave him what warmth and comfort I could. I turned the radio on very softly for him and quite astonishingly it was 'The Nuns' Chorus' from *Casanova*. These were the last sounds that Toby heard.

Some say that they will never have another dog; others that it is best to have another as soon as possible. We agree with the latter, especially if it is possible to get one who needs a home. Babs and I therefore went to the Dogs' Home in Plymouth and were lucky enough to be able to have a black-and-white border collie, just four months old. His nose was still pink and so were his paws. He could as yet only squeak, which he did frequently. Since losing her friend, Cleo had been giving me a great deal of affection, but when Kim arrived on the island her reaction was to leave home. We made up a bed for her in different rooms of the house but she would not settle; for a time she stayed in some comfortable quarters we set up for her in the warm boiler-house under the bathroom, but this did not last for long.

Eventually she worked it out for herself to her own satisfaction; she set up home in the tractor shed. This was about a quarter of a mile away from the house, by the path to the main beach. It was really astute of her, for it had all the conveniences that a cat could desire. It was divided into two by a brick wall, with an entrance through to the back section. On the dividing wall enormous shelves had been built on either side for storing daffodil boxes, fruit baskets, potato sacks and trays, etc. They were about five feet in depth and ran the width of the dividing wall. Her chosen home was not only weatherproof, warm and dry, but from a cat's point of view it was a complete house — a ground floor and, above, two stories and an attic. A ladder was conveniently propped against both sets of shelving so that there was easy access to the upstairs accommodation and the rafters aloft, where planks, tarpaulins and more boxes were stored. Cleo now used the ladder to reach the upper compartment where she made herself a comfortable bed among the potato sacks. We put her meals on the lower shelf which we could reach easily. Cleo would descend the ladder to what had now become her dining-room. This half of the tractor shed faced east and when there was an easterly gale the wind tore through the little opening we had made for her in the barn-like doors, making it draughty. Cleo would then move to the back room of the tractor shed and climb the ladder to the two 'floors' there, which she now used as her temporary bedroom and dining-room, until the gale had subsided, preferring the front section, presumably because she could see all the comings and goings along the path.

In some inexplicable way she now made it known that HamRam, neutered or not, was welcome to her abode. He and he alone was allowed up in her apartments, and visit her he did. Although a big dollopy cat he would climb lightly up the ladder with a swagger and there the two of them would sit for hours. As their two faces peered down at us with the unfathomable way of cats we wondered what attraction they had for each other and we decided, as far as these things can be known by mere humans, that it was a mother and son relationship. HamRam just loved to be pampered and spoiled, and Cleo, as we were to find out later, had a very strong protective instinct. This did not extend to Kim, and for all their lives there was a state of armed neutrality between them that on one unforgettable occasion led to open warfare.

In addition to having bees and a goat we now decided to keep hens. Not only did it seem to fit in with our new life style but we had a ready-made home for them. A short way beyond the tractor shed, in a fenced-in clearing in the woods, was a hen-house in very good condition; lined with straw it would make a very comfortable home indeed — warm, dry and sheltered from gales. We read books on the subject and felt that we, or rather I, should be able to cope. Mrs Alger, a friend and colleague of Babs, heard about this and offered to give us some hens, twelve Rhode Island Reds. As she said that they were getting on in years we imported another twelve of the same breed, but younger. We stocked up with loads of straw and hen food, settled our two broods in and were now, we thought, poultry farmers!

However, as with everything we undertake, we are inclined to see only the advantages. Even with the comparatively straightforward occupation of keeping hens, there are unforeseen snags, especially if they are kept on an island. What if they fall ill or even die on you, for instance? All this and more we were to find out in the future. For the moment we felt we were establishing our roots. We had survived our first daffodil season, the greenhouse was thriving, some of the land was under cultivation, we had a goat, bees and hens, and for recreation we had music, books, a pottery, an embryo darkroom and stone-cutting and polishing equipment — and pets for company.

The leisure activities were still an elusive dream, for ahead of us was a great deal of pioneering before we could even begin to look shipshape.

One of the first decisions to be made when once we had settled in was what to do about the two cottages. Although not exactly derelict they soon would be if we did not do something about them. Not wishing to live with property that would disintegrate and fall down we decided that one of the tasks ahead of us was to put them in order. We would house our friends in them, we said, for holidays and perhaps let them for summer holidays to keep them lived in and cared for. The income from the lettings would pay for their maintenance we hoped — a hope that has, unfortunately, not been fulfilled. Not only is old property notoriously expensive to restore, maintain and service, but the cost of importing labour from the mainland, and the transport of materials over the sea puts the costs up astronomically.

Smugglers' Cottage, the oldest dwelling on the island, and said to date back to the eighteenth century, is a single-storey building and situated in an ideal position. It is protected from the winds by a walled garden in which grow peaches, plums, figs, apples, pears and climbing roses and honeysuckle in great profusion. Inside, however, a black mould clung to the walls and ceilings, the floors were unsafe and one felt in danger of plunging to unknown depths below. We subsequently discovered that they were, like most of those in Jetty Cottage, built directly over the earth. The exception was the hall, which, like part of Jetty Cottage, was floored with concrete. The thought did occur to us that perhaps the treasure was incarcerated under there, but more immediate problems soon chased this fancy away. It was going to be a costly business to restore, decorate and furnish both cottages. Adapting to island life, settling in our own furniture, books and equipment, coping with the generator, the daffodils and trying to develop the market-garden was occupying all our time, so although dealing with the cottages was vital it was not part of our immediate plans.

Now an incident from the past raised itself like a spectre to haunt us. It happened in the previous autumn of 1964, when Babs was working out her term's notice prior to coming down to Cornwall finally at Christmas. I had filled in the time happily, acquiring equipment that I thought would be essential for our island life. High on the list was a portable tape-recorder for the recording of bird song. I finally bought one in the Edgware Road, in a shop bursting at the seams with radios, tape-recorders and all manner of delectable electronic equipment. I say delectable because, although I had no rapport with engines and machinery, the gleaming results of space-age wizardry have a seductive appeal for me, but in truth I did not understand their workings at all, and I was bemused by the dazzling array of equipment set before me. A visiting director of the company was called from the inner office to advise me. The thought did occur to me that perhaps my enthusiasm and maybe the slightly fanatical gleam in my eye had given the assistants the idea that I was going to buy the lot, and the sale deserved to be executed by someone at boardroom level. A very charming and helpful gentleman emerged from behind the scenes, shook hands and described various models to me. Eventually I selected one that he recommended and I reckoned would not be too complicated for my non-electronic brain, nor too expensive for my rapidly diminishing stock of cash. When, during the course of our conversation he heard for what purpose the tape-recorder was to be used and where, he said that he would dearly love to visit us with his family. As he had kindly allowed me 5 per cent discount for paying cash, I felt I could not do otherwise than say that we would be delighted.

So when, in the midst of gathering daffodils, clearing up debris, shingling paths, digging and planting and trying to make some sort of order out of our possessions that were still piled around the place, a letter came from Eric Cox reminding me of our conversation and asking if he and his family could rent one of the cottages, we were non-plussed, to say the least. Never ones to say 'No' when 'Yes', often to our regret, slips more easily off the tongue — or in this case the pen — we wrote and said we were thinking of letting Smugglers' Cottage at some time and we hoped that it would be ready for early June, the time when they wanted to come.

We knew what had to be done and we thought that it was within our capabilities, that is, given the help of a few friends adept at carpentry and plumbing. What we did not realize, and it is a lesson that we still find hard to learn, is the length of time jobs actually take, taking into account all the other demands on our time. We visualize nice blank days for the job in hand, uninterrupted by meals, unexpected happenings and other people's constant needs; we do not reckon either with flagging strength and diminishing enthusiasm as day merges into evening and evening into night.

During the Easter holiday Babs and I started on Smugglers' Cottage. The floor in the sitting-room really needed re-flooring. Where there was an actual hole we stuffed it as best we could, covered it with carpet and put a large piece of furniture on top to prevent anyone from falling through. We could not spend all the time necessary as the daffodil season was late this year and we were still overwhelmed with them and coping with the Easter market. We were also toiling on the land from dawn to dusk whenever possible, that is, when we were not attending to broken-down engines, stopped-up drains, or doling out coffee to chance friends who had come to help. When Babs returned to the mainland after the holiday I continued as much as possible with the cottage. Armed with a basket of sandwiches, wine, baby transistor radio and binoculars for bird-watching and to spy marauders, and equipped with decorating materials, I would set forth for the cottage which was just off the path to the beach and between the orchard and the generator room. I scrubbed, I scraped, I put on undercoat and yet more undercoat, but with other chores accumulating and the hoeing, planting and the greenhouse work it was an uphill battle.

I was glad therefore when Hugh and Kath Gosling came to stay and help. Hugh was the brother of Marjorie Buck who, with her husband Bill, had helped us in settling into our home in No 1 cottage on the mainland in the spring of the previous year, 1964. Hugh was selling his place in Bristol and intended buying an hotel in Cornwall. They had to make several forays before they finally settled on a sixty-bedroomed hotel in Newquay. Each time they spent a few days with us and this was the first of many visits. Their help was invaluable as both could turn their hand to anything. Our rememberance of the indomitable Kath was that she spent the whole of her frequent visits clad in an apron, her head tied up in a scarf and, armed with a paintbrush in one hand and a broom in the other, she always, unbelieveably, had a radiant smile on her face.

Hugh, as well as having expertise in many handyman skills, had practical suggestions to make which helped us enormously, and were a welcome change from some of the far-fetched ones that had assailed our ears from the moment we started on our adventure. He will be remembered especially for three of his many contributions. One was the construction of a rack in the kitchen to store my demijohns of wine. This was built on to the wall and consisted of several shelves some four feet wide and three feet in depth, supported by stout posts on all four corners. It reached from the stone-flagged floor to the oak-beamed ceiling, and when he had stained and finished it, it looked very handsome indeed. Hugh demonstrated that each rack was strong enough to hold at least eight full demijohns by sitting on each shelf as he constructed it; and a funny sight it was to see his sturdy figure when he reached the top shelf, waving his arms, legs a-dangling, bouncing up and down and saying: 'You see! if it will hold my weight it will hold your wine.' Indeed it did, and still does.

Secondly, he mounted two cupboards on the same wall adjoining this edifice. One was a kitchen cupboard we had brought with us, and the other we found on the beach where it

Babs (*left*) and Evelyn, with Lucky. In the background the island with (*l to r*) Jetty Cottage, Island House and Smugglers' Cottage (above Lucky's head)

The island seen from Eastcliff, Looe

Island House and Jetty Cottage, with the mainland in the
background

Jack Tambling, in our boat *the Islander*, off-loading drums of diesel oil which willing helpers roll up to the generator room

Fuel for the Aga being delivered from the Jetty. A calm sea is essential

Babs (*right*) shows Philla the use of the new rotovator – a welcome advance in tilling the soil for the island produce

Clare, one of our regular voluntary helpers, gutting mackerel. Sue looks on, ever hopeful

Evelyn working in her pottery

Babs prawning. Crabs, lobsters, grey mullet, bass and wrasse can also be caught from the island shores

Visitors enjoying tea while Evelyn answers questions about island life in the winter

A party of visitors return to the mainland

Bruce takes evasive action from a gull while servicing the sea-water pump (*see* The Volunteers' Tale)

Hoisting the St George's Flag (*see* The Newcomers' Tale)

Top: 'Dr Livingstone, I presume?'
An important meeting on the
seashore. Babs and Fred
introduce Toby to the new
arrival, Frederica the goat

Centre: Sue, the tabby kitten,
inspects a perfectly preserved
china owl which was washed up
by a gale

Injured birds are often found
around the island. This one is
being fed with cat food

had been brought in by the sea. It was almost identical in size with ours, that is about four feet high and wide. It was in perfect condition structurally but in poor shape aesthetically. Mounting them on the wall at eye level was no problem to him; the touch of genius — and why we always think of Hugh when we use the cupboards — was the finish that he gave to them. He found some battening some three inches wide and he covered the outside of the doors with strips of these. By the time he had fined them down several times, stained and polished them they gave the appearance of rich panelling. The final touch, though, showed his real artistry. On the beach he found parts of our metal boat which had broken up in a storm. From these he cut decorative shapes to form 'wrought-iron hinges'; he then stamped and embossed them all over with a six-inch nail, painted them black and fixed them to the panelled doors, over the existing hinges. This wall was now lined with Hugh's woodwork wizardry. The whole effect was fine indeed, and fitted in with the style of the farmhouse kitchen, giving it an old-world richness and warmth. When the jars were put in place row upon row, one above the other, the scene was one which we were sure the monks of old would have approved of in theory and no doubt appreciated in practice. They gleamed and sparkled in the lamplight from a delicate gold to a brilliant ruby-red, according to their content, and enhanced our kitchen with a patina of jewel-like richness, so that on a dark winter's night it was like entering an Aladdin's cave.

Hugh's third attribute, although vividly recalled, can only be held in our memory. In addition to his many skills he had a hidden talent, that is, hidden from us until he came here; he was able to imitate the cry of the seagull to perfection. He used to roam the island giving his impersonations, much to our confusion, and no doubt, to that of the seagulls too, for wherever he went he was followed by their haunting cries, often rising to frenzied screams. We often wondered what particular significance some of his calls had to evoke these murderous shrieks.

On this, their first visit, they both worked in Smugglers'

Cottage, but even with their help it was not nearly ready as busy week followed busy week. Everywhere, too, grass was growing apace. With the two mowers we brought with us we had five altogether. However, with the rough terrain, the neglect since last summer while the island was uninhabited, and the lack of frost, the island had run wild, and each of the mowers broke down in turn, or more usually lost one of its vital parts in the long grass. Hugh would mend them if possible and then be called away to unstop a drain. Brian and Anne Rainforth, with their two young sons, now returned to help us, so the work-force was growing. In addition, Mr Bray, who owned a carpet shop in Looe, and had come over previously to fix us up with some carpets and lino, said that he and his family would love to help.

On the day the Coxes were due to arrive there were then ten of us working on the cottage: Mr Bray and family were cutting the lawns, the rest of us were frantically putting finishing touches to the paintwork, sweeping out bits and pieces and moving furniture in. In the midst of this, and much to our consternation, Mr Cox and family turned up early. They stood at the gate, no doubt bewildered to see us all beavering away like the seven dwarfs — except that there were ten of us. Doubtless tired from their journey from London and the added chore of heaving themselves and their luggage in and out of a motor-boat, the sea trip, and having to haul everything up from the beach, for of course there was no one there to meet them, the unfortunate Cox family now had brooms and other equipment thrust into their hands, and they had to help push furniture into place before they could take up residence. It says something for their resilience that they have been here many times since and never fail to keep in touch. Such can be the effect of island fever.

So we had our first cottage let and our first cottage income of ten guineas, which I suppose was the going rate at the time. As we had spent a considerable sum in restoring and furnishing the cottage it did seem rather a drop in the ocean, but it was a start, Babs and I told ourselves. We would not have been so sanguine if we could have foreseen that the future maintenance of the cottage would include having the whole flooring, except for the concreted hall, replaced twice, the materials used the first time not having withstood the dampness of the earth foundations.

Putting the Jetty Cottage in order was an even more daunting task. No dwelling likes to be abandoned; when human life no longer breathes therein, the pulse stops and decay slowly sets in. Jetty Cottage had been used as a packing station for daffodils and had not been used as a home for some years, unlike Smugglers' Cottage which had housed the Whitehouse's gardener. Consequently floor-boards, if there were any left, were rotten, and all the earth beneath showed. There was dry rot and wet rot, too; it really was a colossal task ahead of us, but we could not face the prospect of living with mouldering property. It was now that the indefatigable Zena stepped in with the suggestion that her brother, George Marshall, would take on the carpentry, at which he was skilled. The cost would be far less than if we employed a firm, even if there were one willing to send its employees across the sea to work the irregular hours dictated by tides and weather. George did a fine job replacing and making good all the flooring. Perhaps most invaluable of all he ripped off all the wall-panelling, reeking with the deathly smell of wet rot, in the ex-barn/music room that was now our transit camp, and after putting everything in good order refaced the walls with some handsome parana pine panelling. This is a lasting memorial to his skill, for tragically he collapsed and died suddenly while mooring his boat in the harbour at Mevagissey just a few years ago.

Hugh and Kath now added their own special touches to make it habitable once more. Hugh did some of his clever carpentry and panelled round the bath to make a quite elegant splashboard, probably from something dredged up from the sea. Between them they decorated the walls and woodwork of the cottage, which, like Smugglers' Cottage, is all on one floor. They were putting the finishing touches and sweeping out when the boat arrived for their departure from the jetty. Kath stepped on to the boat, still wearing her apron, mob-cap and her engaging smile and as the boat pulled away she threw us a broom which she found she was still clutching.

We had some furniture of our own which we put into both cottages, including some antique chairs and tables, but much more was needed: beds, mattresses, pillows, blankets, carpets, kitchen equipment, crockery, cutlery, lino and much more. Several forays were made to Nancollas's and Hicks's fortnightly sales and to Dingle's, the large store in Plymouth and, with Zena's ever willing help, at last both cottages were fully furnished. Although it had cost us a large sum of money for what was, after all, only one of our projects, we did feel that it was the right thing to do. Not only had we preserved the properties but we had somewhere to accommodate friends and relatives who had hitherto bedded down in odd corners when they came to help us. Among these who now came were Gwen, my friend from the Camera Club days, and Jim Cutts. He had recently returned from abroad and was delighted to try his hand at some quite ambitious carpentry. Thanks to him we have some fine built-in storage cupboards which effectively sealed off the sleeping quarters of Jetty Cottage from the hurly-burly that was continually going on in our transit camp, as furniture was dragged out and other pieces acquired from the mainland were added.

Our niece Cecily, her husband Doug, with their three children Jane, Richard and Manda, now came on holiday to help us. They were still anxious to join us permanently. Doug, a natural craftsman, could turn his hand to anything and, as he could handle boats, would be a great asset. There was much discussion about this for it would be a big step for everyone. Nevertheless they decided that they would like to have a go. So a few months later they joined us.

We started out with high hopes but sadly it did not work out. The main factor was the one we feared when the idea was first mooted — that of economics. As the months went by it became obvious that there was no living and therefore no future for Doug. Mr Whitehouse had told us that the income from the daffodils just about paid the wages of his gardener — around £8 per week. Although we intended to develop the market-garden side there was no way we could see, and neither could Doug, that would provide a living for him and his growing family. The climate was wonderful, the soil fertile and the crops early but with the added cost of sea transport and the uncertainty of getting produce to the mainland for the marketing of the early crops, it was a chancy business, as we had found to our cost with our first forays with the daffodils. It would take years of letting the cottages to repay even the initial cost of making them habitable, without taking into consideration the expensive and continual maintenance that old properties require, and of course, with Doug and family resident in one of them, there would be no income from that one.

So many dream of getting away from it all, and living off the land, or the sea, and being self-sufficient. Many fail and mostly it is a question of economics, which is why, even with their inborn husbandry, the crofters have abandoned so many of the Scottish Isles to make their future on the mainland. St George's is a tiny island, just twenty-two and a half acres. Even if a large amount of capital were injected into it, we doubt it would ever become a viable proposition horticulturally, and any form of commercialism would be quite unacceptable to us. In recent years all the owners have been self-sufficient financially. We too, could sustain ourselves money-wise and we had come here to enjoy island life and develop the island's natural resources; we had no need or wish to make a living from it. But with our commitments: Island House, two cottages, three boats and a generator, together with two cottages and a car on the mainland and our two selves to clothe and feed, there was no way we could also support a family of five, especially as we were both taxed to the hilt as single people without the benefit of family allowances.

Although Doug's help was invaluable it could not add to the island's income in the foreseeable future, and it did not obviate the expense of employing specialist help such as the electrician, the Lister engineer, the plumber and the boat-builder. So although our expenses had increased by providing for five extra people and the heating and lighting of the cottage, our income had not. Financially the future was bleak for Doug, too, as all must find out who opt out of the rat-race for a life of self-sufficiency, especially if they have a growing family. The question of the children's education raised another problem. The Education Authorities paid the ferryman, Leonard Pengelly, for their daily transport to the mainland. The journeys were often rough and, with Manda not yet six, the children were often exhausted after a day's schoolwork followed by a bumpy and sometimes wet journey in an open boat at the end of it. When the weather was too rough in the summer and for most of the winter months, Babs was paid five shillings per head per week to feed and care for them on the mainland. After coming home from a day's teaching with the added responsibilities of her Deputy-Headship it tested her endurance to the limit to have to prepare food for and control someone else's children. It also curtailed her social activities to nil.

Christmas was fun for we had cleared our 'transit camp' enough to use it as a communal room for parties and craft evenings. Cecily did basketry and both she and Doug were keen wood-carvers. The children especially enjoyed the parties.

One party I remember in particular, although it was not held there but in our back bedroom in the house. Manda had decided that I was 'magic'. I had indeed, in my youth, helped our brother, Tom, Cecily's father, with conjuring tricks at children's charity shows. I remembered enough of these to mystify a six-year-old — but not anyone much older — by producing surprise items out of thin air or a nearby bush. Henceforth I was introduced by Manda as 'my aunt — she's magic'. She decided to invite me to a party — the other guests being the Rainforth's children, Mark and Matthew, aged about five and three years. Manda chose our back bedroom for the venue as it would be the most inaccessible to would-be gate-crashers. We all sat in a circle on the floor. Manda had everything set out very nicely, the crockery being a doll's tea-set. Ju-jubes were produced and counted out carefully on to the tiny plates. Orangeade was served in equally miniature cups and saucers with an adult air that would have graced a ladies' tea-party. I did feel a bit like Alice in Wonderland after she had partaken of 'EAT ME' and grown bigger and bigger, especially when I produced my contribution, which was a dish of chips that I had just cooked, for they looked so large beside the ju-jubes. However they were seized on avidly and we were all having a merry time when there was a knock on the door. Cecily poked her head in. 'Have you everything you want?' she asked. Manda dropped her ladylike air and with tea-pot poised in hand screamed: 'GO *AWAY*! *NO* grown-ups allowed!' That cut me down to size!

When they returned to Sussex (for luckily Doug was able to get his job back), Manda came to say good-bye to me. 'You will miss me more than I shall miss you,' she said nodding her head, 'for you will be without me, but I shall have all my friends, so it will be easy for me to forget, but it won't be for you.' I think she was right.

The
WINKLE-PICKER'S
Tale

With the departure of Ruth to help her parents on their smallholding in Looe, in May of our first year, at last came the day when I should be alone on the island.

It is difficult to describe my complex feelings about this. I would, of course, have preferred, more than anything, for Babs to be with me. From the very beginning it had been a joint dream, and in achieving it we had shared the same problems, adventures and dangers. As we experienced the hazards of the sea crossings in mid-winter regretfully we realized that while Babs was teaching it would not be possible for her to live on the island, except for the school holidays and calm weekends; we had come to accept that we should have to live apart for quite long periods.

Babs, of course, could have given up teaching, but this had never come into our calculations. Not only was her income necessary but there was the question of her pension to be considered. Although at that time it was thirteen years away it seemed a very desirable carrot. When we are young a job with a pension seems unutterably dull; something for the old and weary, not for us, the young ones who, of course, will live in our golden adventurous youth for ever. When in mid-stream it is quite a different matter; the idea of being paid for doing absolutely nothing has a compulsive allure, and one is thankful that a pensionable job will bring about this happy state in the foreseeable future. How soon? Without wishing one's life away one yearns for this enticing freedom. How to bring it nearer without advancing towards it?

A badly broken leg from a cliff path fall, combined with increasing responsibilities, pressure of work and the consequent late hours, filled the bill in my case and I retired for health reasons eight years earlier than normal. Although this entailed a reduced pension and the burden of buying National Insurance stamps for that number of years in order to be eligible for the Government Retirement Pension, the fact of having one's day free, and an income however small, gives one a feeling of immense wealth. This is entirely illusory of course — one has to eat, pay the bills and the mortgage. However, a certain amount of illusion is necessary to see one through life if the journey is to be an enjoyable and exciting adventure — a certain amount of illusion and a certain amount of money.

We have often been astonished, not to say appalled, at the number of people who have written to us to say that, as a result of reading about our adventures, they too, have given up everything to start a new life and fulfil long-cherished dreams. I say appalled, for the feeling of responsibility is tremendous. Often we wonder how these folk have made out (and there may be others too, who have not actually written to us). *They* are the brave ones. Many admire us for our supposed courage. This we do not understand for we consider we have been most circumspect. To have been really courageous Babs would have given up her career to enable her to live on the island entirely and we would have tried to live off the land, and be self-sufficient like the pioneers of old, or members of communes fashionable in the last decade or so. As it was, we felt we had been most prudent to decide that an income was necessary. True, Babs had given up her plum job without another in sight, but not even the giddiness of island fever had lured her into giving up her career. Although we had our heads in the clouds we had our feet firmly on the ground too. Admittedly the ground is often slippery, and at times has an uncomfortable habit of giving way under us.

So tacitly we had agreed that until Babs could retire we must accept that she should operate from the mainland. I knew that she was worried about my being alone on the island, and I in turn was concerned that she would not be able to share the full island life for some years to come. But as we had no intention of depending on our own physical efforts and hack out what could only be a meagre existence (for we knew from previous owners that the daffodil farm and market-garden-cum-smallholding needed private means of some sort to keep it going), we felt that we had no choice in the matter.

Thus on this day in mid-May I faced the prospect that in a few hours I should have my first taste of being entirely on my own except for the faithful Toby and the elusive cat.

I must admit to having doubts.

I had never lived alone; had never been too keen even on entering an empty house if the family were out. I was prone to fling doors open suddenly, as in a movie thriller, but without the comfort of the obligatory revolver at the ready. As for venturing to the copse at the end of the garden at dead of night in search of a forgotten book or garden tool, I never went without having Toby by my side held firmly on a lead.

Suddenly I felt nervous and afraid; not of being alone on the island so much, but afraid of being afraid. On the one hand I relished the challenge; on the other I doubted my ability to rise to it.

To add to the ordeal it was raining and a high sea running when at 7 p.m. Peter, Zena and Charles came in the *Islander* to fetch Babs. The jetty was awash and the seagulls screamed in anger at being disturbed in their nests. They take over the rocks on which the jetty is built during the breeding and nesting season, and to avoid being attacked by them at these times we use the landing beach, except when it is too rough to land there as it was this evening. The rain, the high seas sweeping over the jetty and the seagulls dive-bombing with murderous screams did not make our parting easy nor the start of my new life encouraging. Babs looked dejected and forlorn as she clambered into the bucking boat. Zena for once, overcome with the drama of the situation no doubt, was unsmiling beneath her sou'wester and said not a word. As the *Islander* ploughed its way towards the mainland both Babs and Zena looked as though they had just left me condemned to a life of solitary confinement on Devil's Island. Peter and Charles were too busy navigating the boat to register any such fanciful thoughts.

As the boat headed away from me I had a moment of panic; a wave of claustrophobia overwhelmed me. Subject to this in confined spaces, I never expected to experience it on this our dream island with all that space around me. However it was only momentary. Firmly I turned round and marched back to the house.

I would busy myself making some elderflower wine. Soon it was time for the news on the BBC, for running a TV from our generator is one of the luxuries denied to anyone living on a desert island. It was incredibly comforting to have a friendly face telling me the news, and I remember with great affection the kindly Robert Dougall — although I cannot recall a single item of news, if indeed I took it in at the time. To have someone talking to *me*, for such is the intimacy of television, was a terrific boost to my quailing spirit and an anchorage for my floundering thoughts.

I awakened once during the night with a wave of claustrophobia but, when I realized that it was due to nothing more sinister than blocked-up sinuses due to being buffeted by the high winds, I soon fell asleep again.

The next day the weather was still poor with heavy showers so it was not suitable for planting tomatoes as I intended. Keen to occupy myself I put down the elderflower wine I had started, and brewed some beer in readiness for future males who would surely come to help us with the generator, farm machinery and other fearsome mechanical equipment.

Suddenly I realized that I was not afraid at all; it had just been a matter of stage-fright. How could I feel lonely with the faithful Toby by my side, the intriguing cat who was diffidently trying to take up residence now that our visitors had departed, and the island hummed with life — the sea, the gulls, the wind in the trees, the woodland bird song?

My spirits began to soar; it was a great life. As I began to set about all the activities that awaited me — digging, planting, sowing, decorating, pottery, wine-making and the many schemes that we were always thinking up — I began to relish my freedom, freedom from my former life of responsibility for other people, from their demands, the temperamental clashes, the frustrations of their sometimes quite inexplicable behaviour, the irritations and the hurts. No traffic either, and — great joy — no telephones to torment me.

Not even finding a rattish-looking corpse by the gate quelled my buoyant spirits. With an easy rhythm born of optimism I tossed it nonchantly over the cliff with a long-handled Cornish shovel. With luck Babs would be here at the weekend. All was well with the world.

So began a new era in our island saga. Little did I know that during the ensuing years we should have more to do with people of all nationalities, ages, backgrounds, occupations and temperaments than we had ever done in our whole lives — a kaleidoscopic life surely not experienced by the vast majority of people and certainly not to be expected by lone islanders.

In the winter, with storms from the Atlantic sweeping in, Cornwall changes from its summer garb of picturesque fishing villages nestling between green-clad cliffs. Wild seas beat upon the rocky shores from autumn round to spring; the fishing fleet is often harbour-bound for days at a time or even for a week or two. As the island has no harbour it can be isolated for even longer periods. In a south-west gale spray flies over the top of the tall gabled house and lands in great scuds of foam on the lawn. A westerly gale roars through the woods above the house like an express train, deafening one's ear-drums. Forty-feet high trees will be mown down as a hurricane cuts through the woods like a giant scythe; mounds of seaweed pile ten feet high on the beach, so that to reach the *Islander* when the gales have subsided enough for the mail to be brought over it is necessary to slide down these cliffs of seaweed on one's backside. But often gales will assault us again before the sea has died down and the island is virtually like a ship at sea, a little kingdom of its own, dependent on its own resources. On one memorable occasion Babs was unable to land between Christmas and Easter and I just had fleeting glimpses of her as the all-important mail was tossed to me over the raging surf.

In summer it is quite a different matter. For three months when the holiday season is in full swing, although gales and rough seas can be and are a possibility, the sea is most often friendly and full of small craft. The island, as it is only a mile from Looe harbour, is easily accessible when the sea is calm. Mr Whitehouse had warned us about this. 'People will try to land and trespass,' he said. 'To keep your privacy you will have to bring out a shotgun.' Apparently trespassing had been a hazard during the summer months for a very long time. After the war Major General Rawlings, who owned the island then, would let local people picnic on the main beach. The tale we were told was that someone had come up and damaged his greenhouse, so he withdrew the facility and to stop 'uninvited guests' brought out a shotgun to shoot over the heads of would-be intruders. 'This,' said Mr Whitehouse, 'I have had to do too, and so will you.'

I was appalled. For one thing, having spent our first few months on the island in mid-winter and a blustery spring, we did not think that we should have to contend with trespassers. For another I was a 'Master Shot'; I had shot at Bisley for Surrey, and had acquired a goodly number of gold medals, silver cups and other trophies. In fact it was my conceit, still, to go to a handy fair in perhaps Plymouth and relieve the rifle ranges of as much bric-à-brac as I could carry away, for the satisfaction of seeing the astonished faces of the attendants, who had deemed it necessary to show me which end of the rifle to hold, so unlikely a participant did I appear.

'Good Heavens!' I thought, remembering the unerring training on the bull's-eye over the years, 'I won't be able to miss — the beaches will be strewn with dead bodies!'

'Perhaps he is exaggerating,' we said; 'people will respect our privacy' (indicated by the 'Private' and 'NO Landing' notices that were there when we arrived). How naïve we were. As the summer came so did the small boats and land on the island they did.

Before we had to contend with this problem, however, the early part of the season, before holiday-makers abounded, had produced its own special problems. Alone on the island I would espy a beached boat and a figure on the rocks. Down I would saunter to find a 'local'. This presented difficulties. Apparently some people assumed (wrongly) that, being local, they had a right to land, unless of course, as we suspected, they were trying it on with new owners. I, on the other hand, felt that the island was our home, and guests should be by invitation. Confusion arises because it is generally thought that all beaches around the coastline of Great Britain are a free-for-all, and even with beaches that are privately owned the shore below high water is owned by the Crown and therefore the public has free access to it. That may be so generally, but our island is unusual — perhaps unique — in that in 1873 the then Prince of Wales, who later became Edward VII, sold the foreshore rights of the island to settle a gambling debt. This Mr Whitehouse told us. Not only that, he said, but he had had the facts verified legally and had paid a large sum of money to have the rights incorporated in the deeds. 'You must ensure that you keep those rights,' he explained to us, 'for you, too, have paid for their inclusion in the deeds in the purchase price. I went to a great deal of trouble and spent a large sum of money to have the facts verified and legalized.'

So I knew I had right on my side. The difficulty arose with these early intruders in that they were all 'locals'. I did not wish to offend them, for Looe folk had been very kind and hospitable to us as well as helpful in overcoming our pioneering problems. If only I knew who they *were*, but of course I did not. Not being naturally belligerent I decided I would adopt the hostess approach. 'Have we met?' I would inquire pleasantly. Then I would invite him up for a cup of tea, for it was always a 'he' who was the intruder — never a 'she' — and I would dearly like some professor of psychology to explain why. I would then mention the foreshore rights and the difficulties previous owners had had in maintaining them against summer trippers. I hoped to make the point that as far as I knew strangers on our shore might all be summer holiday-makers, and no locals would want, I thought, to be confused with trippers. 'Naturally, as it is our home', I added, 'we like to know who is on our property, and locals like yourself are welcome to visit us and have a cup of tea.'

Mostly this resolved the problem. Once, however, I could

not reach the interloper easily as there was a mass of seaweed-strewn rocks between us. 'Have we met?' I yelled at the top of my voice, not sounding a bit like the gracious hostess I meant to portray. A long string of something that sounded uncommonly like oaths were hurled at me across the rocks, but either due to the distance, the dialect or both, it was all quite unintelligible to me. 'Come and have a cup of tea!' I bellowed. Another string of oaths or whatever. 'We do have foreshore rights and how do I know that you are not just a summer tripper unless you come up and meet me?' I bawled hoarsely. At this he shook his fist at me and made off. Many years later he made himself known to me at some social event. He was a charming man. He recalled the incident; his version being quite different from my interpretation of it at the time. There was no bellicose intent at all, which just goes to show how lack of communication can lead to misunderstandings not only between individuals but between nations.

I was hoist with my own petard on one occasion, however. One morning I noticed on the main beach a rather big and impressive figure, prawning among the rocks. Strolling towards him I used my standard ploy: 'Have we met?' He turned and to my astonishment he said 'We certainly have. I am Mr Wheldon. We met at Mr Nancollas's cocktail party.' I was nonplussed. Mr Nancollas, our agent, had thrown a cocktail party to launch us to the island. The guests were mainly people he thought would be of interest and helpful to us, hoteliers, financiers and the like. Mr Wheldon was one of the latter. I did not recall him, due to the fact, as those who followed our first adventures may remember, that having lived through storms and hazardous crossings during our first few weeks in Looe I was out of training for such sophistication as cocktail parties. The recollection of the party and guests was lost in a rosy haze. 'I was getting some prawns to bring up to you,' he added. This was the first of many visits and he became a regular and welcome guest. We would drink not tea, but coffee and home-made wine. Always he collected prawns, instructing me in the technique of both catching and cooking them. He brought bottles of home-made wine, too, and we drank each other's health and swopped recipes. I really enjoyed his visits.

Much more sinister was an incident that occurred a year or so later. The danger of being invaded out of season is infinitesimal; the seas that pound round the island provide a natural moat. I was astonished, therefore, on a day in early spring, before the locals usually put their boats in the water for the season, to see a lone figure on the rocks below the jetty. I went to investigate. As I came closer I saw a huge fellow crowned with a thatch of yellow hair. I accosted him politely, my heart quaking nevertheless, for it was a giant of a man who looked down at me and he had a Frankensteinish appearance to my heated imagination. I felt no happier when he replied in a thick and almost unintelligible dialect (from outer space perhaps?) that he was winkle-picking and was there any harm in that? Well, there could be. We had heard that a gang of men from 'up country', i.e., beyond the Cornish border, was working its way up from the far west, gathering winkles by the sackful and selling them at inflated prices in London. This was not pleasing to the Cornish and neither, in this particular instance, was it pleasing to me. For one thing the modern and hygienic sewerage system that now services Looe had not then been installed, and the sewage was ejected into the sea at Hannafore. The winkles might well be contaminated. 'Yes, there is harm,' I said, 'people will be poisoned and you will be arrested.' 'Don't you worry about that m'dear. We do this all the time,' he growled in his deep bass voice, and he went on winkle-picking. 'Anyway it is private here,' I retorted. That provoked a lot of 'Ho! Hos!' and some meaningless growlings that ended in a sinister sounding 'm'dear'. But to my intense relief he made off.

The next day, to my consternation, he was there again. My friend and companion at that time was a magnificent border collie, Kim. Kim was most impressive, his fine black-and-white head looking as though he could snaffle a couple of intruders with no trouble at all, and I am sure he would deal with anyone who set about me. The problem was that he was a friendly dog, by nature and by training. He always helped me greet visitors and gave them a warm and doggy welcome. Unless proved otherwise all human visitors were his friends. Why should they be otherwise? I always made everyone welcome. Nevertheless he was an excellent guard dog and he undertook to police the whole island. He would sit on the cliff top outside the house for hours at the 'Red Alert'. He looked right across the bay to the harbour, and quite incredibly would know if it were Leonard's boat, our ferryman at the time, that was leaving the harbour, although there were other similar boats with the same type of petrol-driven engine around, refuting the belief that dogs are short-sighted. Down to the beach he would bound, ready to greet visitors and accompany them up the path to where I was waiting to welcome them. But if any other similar boats came too near into the Jetty bay he would set up such a barking, hurl himself down to the shore and whisk back and forth, still barking ferociously that none dare land.

Indeed it was because of his insistent barking in the house yesterday that I had gone outside to investigate, for some reason leaving him in the house, as I really thought that it must be a false alarm. The problem, now that I intended to take Kim with me, was how to instil into him that I was not greeting a welcome visitor, but without provoking a fracas. Somehow or other I had to assert my authority, with Kim as the implied threat. But there was the rub — I have no authority, unlike Babs, who can summons it up when necessary due to her teaching experience. For instance, if I use a nasty, deep and menacing voice to deter a pet from doing something undesirable, all it does is to come over and lick me or rub against my leg and purr according to its breed, to make me feel better.

So what now? With Kim's proclivity for being friendly to strangers of the 'Have we met?' type, and not wishing to start what might turn into a punch-up or have a knife brandished at me, I decided I would draw on my histrionic powers from amateur acting days. So I put a lead on Kim, which rather puzzled him, then we both marched across the Jetty beach and over the rocks to our winkle-picker. He seemed to look even

bigger than he did yesterday. As we drew near I shortened the
lead and growled in the deepest voice I could muster, 'DOWN!
KIM! *DOWN*!' I then pulled hard back as though I was
restraining him from leaping at the winkle-picker's throat. I
grabbed Kim's collar tight, not only to stop myself from falling
backwards over the rocks but to stop him turning round and
licking me to make me feel better. I smiled apologetically at the
winkle-picker. 'He is a very good guard dog,' I said 'but I will
try to keep him under control,' and I gave another hard pull at
Kim who, hearing my friendly tone, was doing his best to leap
up and say 'Hullo!' I also tried to tuck his wagging tail under
my other arm. 'Down Kim! DOWN! *GOOD BOY*!', I barked.
Well it wasn't really a bark, but it came from somewhere low in
my throat. 'There, I think he will be OK now,' I said, relaxing
my grip a bit, but still pressing hard against his tail with my left
elbow. 'By the way,' I added 'I am afraid that you cannot do any
more winkle-picking here. We have given the franchise to a
local firm. They saw you yesterday and they didn't like it a bit. I
think they are coming out presently to have a word with you.'
He never queried why we had given the franchise for
winkle-picking in a sewerage channel; he never queried why
anyone in their right mind would want it; he never queried why
I had not told him this yesterday. He never queried anything at
all. With hasty glances at Kim he growled, 'Well, I'll be off
m'dear,' and with that he loped with great strides over the rocks
to his boat and rowed hard for the mainland never to be seen
again on our shores.

It was because of this incident and the fact that I would be
alone on the island for about nine months of each year that Babs
applied for, and obtained, a licence from the GPO for the use of
a radio telephone with our own wavelength. This not only gave
Babs peace of mind but it was a facility that was to prove
invaluable to us and to others over the years.

The
COOK'S
Tale

The onset of the holiday season of our first year presented us with a problem that was to affect the whole of our future island life.

In the summer visitors come to Looe in their masses and the bay teems with craft. Small motor-boats, locally called 'doodle-bugs', are hired out and officially are not allowed to land anywhere. The attraction of the island, however, had often proved too great and they, and other privately owned boats, landed as Mr Whitehouse had warned us they would. To have strangers roam around our garden, for that is what the island is to us, and perhaps peer through our windows was too much to contemplate. One might as well live in a goldfish bowl.

To quote an immortal phrase: 'Something must be done'.

I hit on the idea of giving the impression that the island was populated with vast numbers of residents hostile to strangers, for I was sensitive to the fact that there was only one human in residence — myself — to cope with what might well become a population explosion of trespassers. To this end I picked up a couple of anoraks, an oilskin, two sou'westers and an assortment of woolly hats. At the first sign of small boats approaching I peered over the hedge on the cliff top by the house, glaring as fearsomely as I could. I then ducked down, donned a hooded anorak, glared again, ducked, changed to a sou'wester and so on, ducking, changing and glaring until my supply of headgear was exhausted. Then, gathering up all my props, I raced down the path until I found a suitable gap in the hedge on the cliff edge there, and repeated the performance. I hoped that I had given the impression that at least twenty angry people were awaiting any intruders. It must have been successful for all the little boats, without exception, turned back and made for the harbour.

The next day, at the first sign of approaching boats I gave a repeat performance, adding an assortment of garden tools and the odd fishing net to my props and throwing in some extra grimaces as an encore. For the second day there were no intruders and the boats all made back for the harbour. I was, however, exhausted and decided that there were too many other things to do than use my time and energy giving one-woman stands on the cliff top, successful though they had been.

Babs and I discussed the matter at the weekend. Of all the problems we had expected to face in coming to the island — hunger, hardships, privations, storms — yes, but invasion — never. Back and forth we tossed ideas. Suddenly I had an inspiration. 'I've got it!' I shouted.' We will put up a big notice "Landing fee" that will stop them.' Simple. Brilliant. Babs thought it a splendid solution. How much? At that time the going rate for stately homes was 2s. 6d. entrance fee. We would do the same and become a stately island. The only difference being that we were trying to keep people away not inducing them to come.

Triumphantly we nailed a large piece of wood beneath the 'STRICTLY PRIVATE' notice and painted in bold letters 'LANDING FEE 2s. 6d.' — a challenge to any would-be trespassers.

How wrong can you be? Obviously I had never studied psychology nor did I have any inkling about human nature, or I should have realized that the very fact that there was a charge made it appear that to land was attractive and desirable. It is also common knowledge that anything that is free is thought of as having little worth; that the more you pay the more value the object appears to have. Unfortunately I did not have this common knowledge, nor did common sense tell us that we were in fact issuing an invitation to any passing craft if the passengers were prepared to pay.

And care to pay they did. Back in Looe Babs heard that the word had gone around. Looe folk were saying: 'How wonderful!

at last we can visit that lovely island officially, *and* we can send our visitors there.' For like all guest-house owners, they liked to have local attractions to suggest to visitors, who invariably ask on arrival in a district new to them; 'What is there to do? Where to go?'

Alone in my splendid isolation, bringing up shingle for the main path—a wearisome task, but essential if we were not to be bogged down in a morass of mud—I so far knew none of this. A day or so later, dressed in old jeans and a fisherman's smock, I was astonished to see four people marching up the path each brandishing a half-crown a-piece. 'You must be the owner,' they said, thrusting the half-crowns into my hand. 'May we have a cup of tea?' 'Certainly,' I stuttered, not knowing what to say or do. I could not very well say 'Get off my island!', for there was the landing fee notice and here in my unwilling hand was a fistful of coins. To gain time to think I put on my best hostess voice. 'Perhaps you would care to walk round the island while I put the kettle on,' I invited. And to my relief off they went.

Presently there was a knock on the door. 'Oh! do come in,' I said. I ushered them along to the sitting-room, chock-a-block with books, overspilling the bookcases. 'Make yourselves at home.' I shut myself in the kitchen. While they had been walking around the island I had quickly knocked up some scones and baked them to a golden brown in our now ever-ready Aga. Did they actually *want* scones? Should I be a waitress and don an overall? Did they expect to *pay*, if so how much should I charge and would I get a tip? What should I do with it if I did get one, or what? especially or what? In the end I loaded up the tray with the tea, scones, butter and jam, donned a pretty apron which could pass muster as that worn either by a waitress *or* the owner of an island, and sailed into the sitting-room. As I stood there with the tray held in front of me like a battering ram, so confused was I in my mind that I remember asking myself, for no reason at all, 'Is this a sitting-room? If so what does one do in all the other rooms in a house — stand?' We had migrated from a drawing-room at Epsom Downs, but it had not bothered us that we had never practised the graphic arts there, nor

withdrawn to it; this suggesting an elegance of movement
reminiscent of Jane Austen, and hardly applicable to our
whirlwind life there. This room here had been handed on to us
as a lounge, but to anyone who knows their Mitford, this is a
quite dreadful word unless you happen to be residing in an hotel
or loitering in an airport — or is it? — and if so do we really
care? All we knew was that we never had the time to sit or lounge
here — our longest sojourn having been the night we arrived
when we had slept on its bare boards.

This however was no time to consider socially acceptable or
apt nomenclature. As these stupid and irrelevant thoughts
buzzed through my head, the more pertinent question arose as
to what attitude I should adopt. Should it be deferential?
autocratic? nonchalant? welcoming? Suddenly the incongruity
of the situation overcame me. Putting the tray down on the
nearest table I burst out laughing. Between gales of mirth I told
them my nail-biting problems. Bless their hearts — they all
joined in the merriment! I flung off my apron, sat down with
them and we all had tea together. They were two charming
couples. One worked in a West Country brewery and promised
to send me some hops for my beer brewing. He was as good as
his word. In fact a week or two later gifts and appreciative letters
arrived from both couples.

Delightful as this episode was it was obvious that we had
another problem on our hands — two problems in fact. The
first, apparently insoluble one, was the fact that people could
land if they paid, and there was nothing we could do about it all
the time our notice was displayed. We could, of course, do a
volte-face; I could emulate the General and Mr Whitehouse by
making a trio of owners who manned the guns to guard their
privacy; revert to performing antics on the cliff top, or we could
accept the intrusions gracefully. The second problem was that,
if we did allow people to land, there would arise the question of
providing tea. We were now realistic enough to face the fact
that most folk, after making the boat trip and climbing around
the island, would want a cup of tea. It had never been an
ambition of ours to run a café. Babs was possibly better con-

ditioned temperamentally than I was to do so. She was used to organizing fêtes, Leisure and Career Exhibitions and charity functions. Refreshments were endemic to all of these. To provide the same facilities on the island, even if she were here to do so, would be a busman's holiday. She saw her island-life interludes of the school holidays as a kind of ex-curriculum of school activities. For myself I knew how I felt and I had every reason to fear catering for other people.

During my career in the WRNS, although it was not my wish, it was entirely my own fault that I became involved in catering. Also against my wishes, I had been detailed to train for 'Admin', and to this end was posted to Scotland prior to being sent to Greenwich Naval College to be commissioned. A visiting Superintendent WRNS decreed that I should have 'port' experience before attaining the giddy heights of becoming an officer in the WRNS. Consequently I was packed off to Dover. Here, to my chagrin, I found that I was doing exactly the same sort of work in the same sort of office as I had in Scotland. Except for the shells whizzing overhead from France and the bombs being dropped from enemy aircraft above, it was just a replica of the Regulating Office at Balloch on the shores of Loch Lomond.

I asked for an interview with the Chief Officer-in-Charge. I explained to her that if I were going to be in charge of Wrens I reckoned that I ought to have some experience of their jobs at first hand. Could I please be assigned to each of the different categories to gain the necessary experience. The Chief Officer was non-plussed. Highly irregular. Not quite the thing. Some jobs too menial for a Petty Officer. She would have to think about it. Think about it she did, for within a short time I was sent for; it had been agreed and a curriculum would be made out for my entire stay in Dover, embracing all the Wrens' categories. Where they were too technical, like radar for example, I would just 'sit in'; at the rest I could have a go.

It proved to be most educational. As an officer's steward I cleaned out cabins, changed linen and pressed suits all day long and saw not a soul, for the occupants of the cabins were all out waging their bit of the war. A lonely job and, as I later discovered from some of my colleagues, rather looked down upon by a few of the 'Writer' class, albeit at one time titled ladies had taken on some of these lowly jobs in their keen desire to serve their country in the Navy.

When I did my stint in 'Supply' I was welcomed with open arms by the male Chief Petty Officer. 'They *will* send me Wrens who are good at Maths and they are all small girls,' he moaned. 'What I need are strapping lasses who can reach the top shelves and are strong enough to heave boxes of boots and heavy equipment around. *I* can do the sums.' I looked at his smart but undeniably petite Wrens and duly made a note of his complaint. I have often wondered if this aspect of the war has changed and perhaps even to this day the Supply Department or its modern equivalent is staffed by giant six-footers capable of heaving heavy boxes from the top shelves, or whether it is still manned by the dainty type of Wren Einsteins of yesteryear.

Next I drove round the harbour with the M/T drivers. This was hair-raising as, with great expertise, they reversed to the edge of the quayside to disgorge their goods. I learned from this that Wren M/T drivers certainly have to keep their cool! It also got me an invitation on board an MTB. Here I was entertained by the Officer I/C in his minuscule Wardroom, and I was allowed to drive the craft round and round Dover harbour at great speed. This was very exciting; the only disappointment was that it was forbidden to go outside the harbour. This was probably due to the danger of marauding enemy submarines or perhaps our own minefields. I never knew.

I was allowed to sit in on highly top secret technical operations where Wrens worked, incarcerated in the bowels of the earth. I was sworn to secrecy and warned that, to my dying day, I was never to reveal *anything* that I had seen. Whether it was fear of bringing this day nearer by so doing or the effect of the naval tradition of 'sealed lips' inculcated in one I do not know. I do know that as a result I must have given myself a mental black-out, for, though I can remember minute trivia of those Dover days, that visit is a complete blank and to this day I cannot recall a single thing that I saw nor the secret destination to which I had been taken.

Cooking was another matter entirely. Here I was in my element. No matter that I had to be on duty at 5 a.m. and chop frozen meat, pound after pound after pound, until my fingers were frozen too. Cooking fulfils a basic urge; it is creative, artistic — a craft. One is Mother Earth bestowing the largesse of nature to feed the hungry and succour the weak. Or so I thought.

'Forty omelettes for dinner tonight!' ordered the Chief Petty Officer Wren Cook. Dutifully I beat up gallons of reconstituted dried eggs. I beat with a will for hours until I had pitchers overflowing with bubbling froth. They were left to settle until the evening then beaten again. I did my very best — that I should never see the recipients mattered not at all. When the time came for cooking I had the frothiest mixture you ever did see. The golden liquid slid into the pan and a few moments later — behold a perfect omelette! But I had to do this forty times. 'Hurry!' commanded the Cook, 'the first ones have finished and want more and the others have not had any yet.' I hurried. The heat became intense as I toiled away. Frozen fingers at 5 a.m. and now on the verge of a heat stroke. The more I made the more they wanted. By the time I had cooked sixty my strength and the dried egg mixture had given out. Elated with congratulatory messages that came back from the Wardroom I staggered from the galley eventually, exhausted but triumphant.

The next day the Chief PO Cook sent for me. 'You are wasted in "Admin",' she announced, 'I am going to recommend that you change your category to Cook.' I looked at her aghast. Reaction had set in. I never wanted to see another omelette again in my life. I was fed up with chopping frozen meat at crack of, or before, dawn, for I had been at it again that morning and I no longer had any desire whatever of being Mother Earth. In any event I only wanted to find out what it was like to be a cook. I now knew it was unremitting hard work in conditions ranging from Antarctica to the Equator.

Somehow or other I left Dover without changing to cook, but it was this skirmish with cooking that later involved me in catering, again carried away by my own enthusiasm.

Soon after this I was posted to Greenwich Naval College, obtained my commission in 'Admin' and, after three months up North as assistant to a Chief Officer WRNS, was sent as a matter of urgency to take up the post of Officer I/C WRNS at Cookham Camp Signal Station near Chatham. Due to the fact that it was only a small unit of 150 Wrens I was the sole WRNS Officer. On the face of it I had been selected to fill this sudden vacancy, although so newly commissioned, because of my experience of having a go at everything. Hoist with my own petard I now found that I was in charge of everything and that included catering. I soon discovered, as everyone does who has anything to do with feeding people, that they will *complain* — even in wartime. Heroically they will put up with bombing, black-outs, shortages, parting with loved ones, but food not to their fancy they will *not*. The Wrens did not complain about their food — not exactly. The daily allowance was 1s. 5d. per head. Food could be drawn entirely from Naval Stores if one wished, but I preferred to do some prudent shopping around by telephone. Soon I had quite a circle of shopkeepers in Chatham who would ring up if they had anything that was in short supply or was going cheap.

On one occasion it was highly embarrassing. The CO, in his splendid gold braid, accompanied by the First Lieutenant and the Supply Officer, paid me an official visit in my office. Somewhere in the camp a typewriter had gone missing. There was to be an official inquiry. Would I please organize a search of the Wrens' Quarters. All three towered over me. You would think that a flotilla of HM Navy had disappeared at sea without trace. At that moment the phone rang. It was the fishmonger. 'I have some bloaters in. Would you like some?' he asked excitedly. 'Certainly,' I replied crisply, trying to sound as if I were talking to the Chief Officer WRNS, Chatham. 'How many would you like?' he continued, 'I don't often get them offered to me.' 'As many as you can manage,' I replied; '*Thanks* most *awfully*,' dropping the usual conspiratory tones in which we usually spoke to each other. I put the phone down. The CO paused in mid-stream. Was I perhaps increasing my quota of Wrens without his knowledge or permission? I was always demanding more. Luckily he did not take me up on this, as he was too worried about the missing typewriter, for which I was thankful as I was not sure whether he would approve of my shopping locally instead of drawing from naval stores. As a matter of interest the typewriter was eventually found in separate parts, distributed in various drawers throughout the camp. So the quaking culprit was never found nor had to face a court-martial. As for the bloaters, the Wrens were able to feast royally on them in various guises for days on end, although it *is* hard to disguise a bloater indefinitely. No, the Wrens did not complain about a surfeit of bloaters.

This prudent shopping around enabled me to save money on the 1*s.* 5*d.* per head allowance. With the willing co-operation of the Chief PO Wren Cook I was able to provide three cooked meals a day plus a mid-morning snack, tea and cake in the afternoon and hot cocoa and another snack at bedtime. And I had money over. This provided luxuries like strawberries when in season and other delicacies and a reserve fund for providing refreshments at parties and dances to which naval ratings were invited.

You would think that I would be the heroine of the war — Cookham Camp. Not on your life. First a Wren requested an interview, representing, she said, several other Wrens, for she knew that a deputation would, according to King's Regulations, be classed as a mutiny. Instead of spending it on food, please could there be a share-out among the Wrens, of the money saved. Also they didn't see why the naval ratings should benefit. 'Perhaps you would like the dances cancelled,' I offered. 'No, the Navy should provide those, we just want a share-out.' 'That is quite impossible — it is Navy money intended for food and must be spent on food.' She had to accept this decision but was not a bit happy about it. The Chief P.O. Cook assured me that it was only a small number of Wrens who wanted a share-out; the majority were highly satisfied. Nevertheless I was quite chastened, for this budgeting took a considerable amount of my spare time.

Next I had another visit from the CO. The naval ratings, he told me, had started to complain. 'Why', they asked, 'were the Wrens being better fed than we are?' 'I think I should send the Supply Officer to see you,' said the CO; 'the men are complaining so I shall have to do something about it.' 'I don't think that is necessary,' I said in alarm. I did not want any gate-crashing into my coterie of shopkeepers and I did not think that a naval Supply Officer would be too pleased at having to seek my advice. 'The reason is that it is so much easier to cater for 150 than a 1,000 or so. Apart from that, men eat far more than girls. It must be very difficult.' Hoping to divert him I threw in my own complaint: 'According to the Naval quota I am only allowed one and a half cooks for the number of Wrens in my Unit and I need three — one for each watch.' He looked aghast. 'Whatever do you do?' 'Use half an officer's steward,' I replied, 'and work two watches instead of three, but it is not very popular and overworks the cooks.' 'Well write to the Admiralty and I will endorse it,' the poor man said and left. In due course I got my three cooks, so some good came out of the visit.

A day or so later a naval rating messenger appeared at the door. 'The Commander sends his compliments and would you be so good as to come and see him at your early convenience.' Although politely couched, as in true naval fashion, this meant: 'This is urgent. Come at once!' 'It is the Wardroom now,' he said. 'They want you to do the catering for them.' Would I please therefore be the Honorary Catering Officer for the Wardroom. The steward in charge did not think very much of this idea. And neither did I. I ate in the Wardroom myself. As the only woman among so many naval officers I received special treatment — the CO for instance, a highly moral gentleman, would not allow swearing in my presence. If an officer let drop so much as one 'bloody' he was made to apologise, and of course I was never wanting for an escort to dances, concerts and parties down in Chatham. Their ages ranged from veterans of the Battle of Jutland to young midshipmen, and we all lived in happy accord. Until now. At every mealtime I became the butt of all their complaints and suggestions. 'Made-up dishes again! Why can't we have roast meat?' Very soon I discovered that all men want for lunch and dinner is a cut off the joint and two veg., or fish and chips, day after day, after day. It did not matter that there was rationing, they knew what they wanted; the rest was my affair. The only mealtimes I could enjoy, with happy faces around me, was when I could supply their beloved roast, steak and kidney pie or pudding or fish and chips. It was a wonder the war went on at all with all this preoccupation with food. I often wondered if the Nazis were at it, too, on their side of the Channel, and if they spent all *their* time arguing about their wurst and sauerkraut or whatever, and, if so, how they ever had time to come and fling their bombs at us. No wonder Hitler had to invent pilotless planes.

So the last thing I wanted in our island paradise was to be involved in catering.

All these recollections went through my head as I toiled away at lugging shingle up the path and hacked away at overgrown verges until Babs should come again to discuss these pressing problems. 'Perhaps', we said, 'a local firm or family would come over and run a tea-shop or café during the summer.' 'Not a hope,' said Mr Nancollas. 'With the tides, the wind and the weather to contend with and the short season there would be no hope of making it pay, far less make a profit. In fact they would lose money in no time at all. Nobody would take it on.'

Meantime, with the problem still unresolved, more and more people were marching up the path clutching their half-crowns. Not many. Only small groups but to me it seemed like an army on the move. I managed to contain the situation, until one day twenty-two visitors arrived at once and they all wanted coffee. I did not have twenty-two coffee cups but managed with an assortment of mugs and teacups. Then they all wanted lunch — at the same time — 1 o'clock. 'OK', I quavered. Hastily I pulled some lettuce from the garden. Opened a tin of ham. Tomatoes? Yes. Fruit? I could make a fruit salad if I opened some tins as well. There was some cream Babs had brought for me at the weekend. But what about plates? I only had six. No one would understand. Earlier, when we had twenty friends staying on the island to help us, they were parked out in the cottages and we provided them with eggs to have boiled for breakfast. We dished out egg boxes. 'Just cut them up, they make very good egg cups,' we said. Well they would wouldn't they? That is what they had been stored in. 'Good gracious!' they cried: 'Didn't you have any egg cups before you came here?' 'Of course,' we replied tartly. 'Six was quite enough for the two of us. We hadn't twenty — have you?'

So I knew that no one would understand that you do not start off life on an uninhabited island complete with a dinner service including twenty-two dinner plates. Around 1 o'clock they started to stream in. I served the first six. I then engaged the next party in conversation while, out of the corner of my eye, I kept watch on the progress of Party No. 1. This was not too difficult. Visitors love to ask questions. All I had to do was stand there. 'What is it like in the winter?' 'How did you come to own an island in the first place?' 'What about electricity? fresh water? stores? Suppose you are ill? — are you ever *frightened*?' It was like holding a press conference. This questioning goes on to this day and it has convinced me, too, that I am useless at café work. Babs is much more adept than I am. As she is a teacher it comes naturally to her to do at least two things at once. I admire the way she can load a tray, make tea, take money, give change, and converse charmingly, all seemingly at the same time. If I am in the same situation, if anyone asks me for instance 'What is it like in the winter?' I tell them, giving them my undivided attention. This may be rewarding to the questioner but it does mean that the tea gets cold or is not in the pot at all, or some baffled customer finds a blob of jam but no scone on his or her plate. I cannot give change either, for the same reason. In any case I have never become used to the new money. I rarely go ashore and have never been accustomed to handling cash. I have always been a cheque person, as this leaves one's financial state comfortably in the dark. To me a 10p piece will always be 2s. As this means that everyone will get short change I ask people to count it out for themselves, and that leaves me free to answer questions. In fact, in the café I am reduced to a gibbering fool.

Today, however, my ineptitude served me in good stead. As soon as the munching ceased I detached myself from Group No. 2, raced back to the house with the dishes, washed and wiped them at great speed, set out the salad as artistically as I could, then, at the disjointed speed of the old silent films I pelted back at breakneck speed, pulling myself up short, like a Keystone Kop, at the last moment so that I could saunter in with some semblance of efficient calm. Party No. 3 was kept at bay by the same technique, but knowing that I could not bring off the ploy a third time I just did not appear at all, but lurked behind the scenes until the second lot of munching ceased. Luckily Party No. 1, who were awaiting their fruit salad and cream, got into conversation with Party No. 3. Party No. 4 was late anyway. Incredibly everyone was fed, and I persuaded myself that, with the talking going on, no one realized that they were all eating at different times and from the same plates. Not having any idea of what to charge I said the first thing that came into my head, which was 1s. 6d. per head. They all seemed very pleased and asked if they could have tea later. After this was served, which was a simple operation compared with the lunch-time marathon, they all thanked me profusely and went home. They had had a lovely day — the highlight of their holiday — they all said. Well, my highlight was that although I had served twenty-two people on three occasions, at the end of the day I only had six of anything to wash up.

As I crawled into bed that night 'had we', I asked myself 'attained the almost impossible in acquiring our very own island merely to give strangers a lovely day; our crowning success to be left with a minimum of washing-up?' As I dozed off, sleepily I murmured; 'who is the Potter, pray, and who the Pot?'

Babs and I would have to hold another emergency meeting.

The
VOLUNTEERS'
Tale

We decided to seek the help of the National Trust.

The area representative came to see us, made a tour of the island and said that in his opinion if the National Trust owned the island they would have to commercialize it to make it pay. That is, he said, they would have to build a number of holiday chalets and other facilities and probably convert the tractor shed into a cottage, in order to bring in enough income to pay a warden, his wife and staff. Unlike their mainland properties, the season when the island could be open to visitors would be very short and then would be restricted by tides and weather. He could not see it as a viable project. Nevertheless he wished us luck and said that, of course, the National Trust would encourage us in our endeavours.

Impasse! Back to the drawing-board. So far crowds of friends and relatives had come to stay at intervals during the holiday period helping us in every possible way. This was fine as far as maintaining the island was concerned, but if we were to allow people to land and to provide refreshments for them we should need more continuity of help. Soon after this visit from the National Trust, but whether as a result or not we did not know, we had a letter from the then Conservation Corps (now The British Trust for Conservation Volunteers). It said in effect that they would help by writing about us in their magazine and encourage voluntary help, as we were doing a splendid thing in opening the island to visitors. Our spirits rose; mentally I packed away my mythical shot gun and performances on the cliff top.

Did we want to do this? Babs had no doubts. 'With this encouragement we *should* share this lovely place with others,' she exclaimed enthusiastically. 'I am sure it is the right thing to do.' Inwardly I groaned, for Babs is far more public-spirited than I am. I saw my splendid solitude slipping away from me — this balm to my spirit evaporate before it had time to work its healing powers.

Longingly I began to dream of an island far away — in the Pacific perhaps — where no one could get at us. But I knew what would happen. Natives would land from neighbouring islands, for as soon as we took up residence, our island would appear to them to be much more desirable than their own. Should we be foolish enough to try to guard our privacy by putting up a notice saying, for instance, *LANDING FEE — 10 COCONUTS*, it would be the signal for an air-shuttle service from places as far away as China and Japan to disgorge posses of people, demanding chow or sake or whatever. No! there was no escape. It was meant to be. Just as by an extraordinary chain of coincidences we had been brought to this enchanting island, so now it seemed we were destined to open it and share it with others. Destiny did not indicate anything about sharing the bills; probably that aspect was not within its province, but it saw to it that we would be helped in other ways.

Over the years we have been greatly encouraged by the enormous amount of goodwill and help that we have received, so often from complete strangers. Some will give donations, some gifts and others will toil unceasingly to help us. Many have become our friends. One lady regularly sent us a cheque for £100, when this was worth much more than it is today. As a business woman, she said (we heard later that she owned a five-star hotel) she knew how worthwhile projects such as ours foundered and had to be abandoned for lack of financial support.

Day visitors write us letters of thanks and send us photographs and presents. Professional artists have given us paintings of the island, sometimes beautifully framed. One couple, whose interest is folk singing, composed a song about us and the island, included it in their repertoire and made a recording for us. We are encouraged not only by our own countrymen in our endeavours. Even this very day as I write, in

a temporary lull in the autumn gales, over the empty sea came
two people, ferried by our present charming and indomitable
ferryman — Dick Butters in his *Summer Star*. In fact there were
three passengers — a German with his wife and one-year-old
baby. Nineteen years ago, he told us, he had as a youth rowed
here all the way from Polperro. We had made him welcome and
tended his blisters. He had never forgotten the island or us.
Now, a married man of forty, he had flown over from
Baden-Baden for a five-day visit to Looe especially so that he
could come to see us. He came laden with gift-wrapped presents
for us all the way from Germany — liqueur chocolates in a
hand-made basket and another with chocolate-covered marzi-
pans enclosing more liqueurs surrounding a beautifully decorated china dish.

In face of such touching tributes what can one do? To be
honest, as we never wanted to open the island in the first place,
we are often tempted to close it again. We came here to enjoy
island life, not on the one hand to make a living nor on the other
to be a public service by providing an oasis of tranquility and
beauty for others. Inexorably we found ourselves becoming a
public service in spite of our insular ambitions. That nothing
would tempt us to spoil or commercialize the island by so doing
put us on a suicide course.

The Conservation Corps, however, were as good as their word
and soon we had applicants for our working holidays. As so far
little was known about us we asked the Students' Union to
mention our working holidays in their magazine too. We
probably cast our net too wide, for not only did we get
applications from dedicated conservationists and students
genuinely desirous to help and practise their skills, but it also
encouraged those who merely wanted to fill a gap between digs
and others who saw only the glamour of life on an island and
were not prepared for any hard grind.

The first mistake we made was to provide accommodation,
gas, electricity and food which we cooked, all without any
charge, in exchange for their work. It seemed a reasonable
arrangement in theory. In practice it was quite a different

matter. Most of the volunteers at that time were students. No one coming our way showed any signs of anorexia — they all had enormous appetites. Catering for up to eight helpers was like being the mother of a large family of teenagers who were at home all day long. With no maternal instinct and not very much in the way of emergency stores, I found that once again catering was raising its head like a leering ogre.

I remember one helper in particular. He fancied himself as an artist and assumed the so-called artistic temperament. He was the only volunteer at the time, as it was early in the season when no other students were free to come, and his help would have been invaluable. It did seem to me however that he just passed the time between one meal and the next, although in a very charming manner. One day I was beavering away shifting coal and digging trenches for potatoes, when he strolled up to me. I forget what particular job he had been allocated, but whatever it was he was obviously not doing it. 'I feel rather guilty', he said 'seeing you working so hard. I haven't done anything this morning as I didn't feel like it. I have been sketching instead. I do hope you don't mind.' I rested on my spade for a moment. 'That is perfectly all right,' I said. 'You will understand, of course, that I may not feel like cooking the meal tonight as I have a poem I want to finish.' He was a decent chap though and after that he did buckle to — and his sketches were really quite good.

Some students were fussy beyond belief. 'Would you please make a meat pie with onion at one end only!' asked one. 'I do not eat peaches, oranges, apples, rice, fish, poultry, cream, green vegetables, butter or bread,' said another, 'and I do not care for potatoes,' he added, 'unless they are chips.' 'What *do* you like?' I asked, trying to keep the menace out of my voice. 'Practically anything else. My mother knows exactly what I want,' he replied. I bet she did, but why didn't she give it to him? I very nearly did! 'Please do not serve anything wrapped in pastry,' said one. 'Meat pies only,' requested another. 'No meat of any kind,' insisted a third, 'only ham, fish or poultry.' 'I'm a vegan,' announced another.

I was getting quite demented, for one of the things that some of them did not care for either was work. I was having to fit in this frustrating catering for helpers with attending to visitors, working on the land and in the greenhouse and trying to supervise any work that was being done. Of course some were very good, worked hard and have kept in touch with us over the years, but there was no way of knowing beforehand what the intake of helpers was going to be like and what kind of food to get in.

At one of our many weekend board meetings Babs and I decided that the only answer was for the helpers to do their own cooking. We would supply the food and make a rota for 'Cook of the Day'. But this did not work for the simple reason that some of them could not cook, or even worse, jumped at the chance of having a go. One young girl said that her mother would never allow her to cook at home, although she loved it and she could do a very good soufflé. Could she have a go? I was intrigued. I would love to know the secret of a good soufflé. She asked for nine eggs. I quailed, for that would leave me with only three for their breakfast, and the dish was to provide a lunch, not an evening meal. However I produced the nine eggs and waited, for I was to share in this gourmet delicacy. Presently we were served with a perfectly respectable omelette apiece. Everyone was delighted and congratulated the proud cook. 'Now,' they said 'what are we having for lunch?' I now know why her mother would not let her cook at home. She couldn't afford it.

It was during this period that I came face to face with Women's Lib, which was then enjoying its great upsurge. To make our position 'absolutely clear', as the politicians say (I have often wondered what *is* clearer than clear?), Babs and I reckoned that we had liberated ourselves decades ago, long before it became fashionable. We had thrown off the shackles of domesticity without depriving men of their rightful role in life, which was looking after us. This was not part of a movement as far as we were concerned, for we believed in the right person for the right job.

Not so one of our helpers; she was a wisp of a girl, a young student, and an ardent Women's Libber. Now if the 'Cook of the Day' happened to be a fellow and he could cook — and some of them were very good cooks indeed — all was well, but if he was not, there was always some girl willing to volunteer in his place. When it came to Basil's turn, who had never cooked in his life before, our Women's Libber insisted that he do his stint and she would do his job of chopping up some enormous logs. Basil, a tall gangling youth, dutifully turned up in the kitchen for provisions and instructions. 'Is there anything you *can* cook?' I asked. 'Well, I can make a blancmange,' he replied. 'OK', I said, 'I will cook the main dish, steak pie and vegetables. You can serve it up and then produce your blancmange and fruit. That way it will appear that you have done the lot.' In a short time he had made the blancmange and put it in the fridge to set. When the pie was cooked and everything was ready to be dished up I took the blancmange out of the fridge ready for Basil to turn it out. To my horror it had not set at all — it was as runny as milk. 'How did you make it?' I asked. 'Just as the instructions said,' he replied, 'I mixed the powder with the milk.' 'Didn't you bring the milk up to the boil?' I asked. 'Oh no! I mixed it with the cold milk and put it in the fridge.' In desperation I heated up vast quantities of gelatine, stirred it into the liquid blancmange and thrust it back into the fridge; Basil went off in triumph with the steaming pie, its golden crust topping the succulent mixture beneath, and by the time the helpers had eaten their way through that, by some incredible luck, the blancmange had set. The little Woman's Libber, all hot and flustered, was almost too tired to eat hers. 'I couldn't manage the chopping,' she gulped — 'it was just too much for me.'

The next day Basil was on duty in the café. I happend to be there and was the witness to a scene that I shall never forget. There stood Basil, his gangling figure towering above a table of ladies he had just served with tea, scones and jam. 'And do you know,' one of the ladies called over to an adjoining table, 'he does all the cooking here as well!' There stood Basil with a look of ineffable pride on his face, for I am quite sure he felt as if indeed he had done so.

All in all this catering became a huge burden. I seemed always to be involved one way or another with the cooking of the evening meal. Each 'Cook of the Day' had one day of the week on duty. When the day visitors left all other helpers were off duty for the evening and would then go swimming or whatever, while I perforce was on duty every evening. When the meal was finally finished and I had made sure that I was not left with greasy pans hidden in odd corners, the next day's 'Cook of the Day' came up for provisions for breakfast, lunch and so on. After doing the day's accounts and answering knocks from helpers and cottagers, 'now that you are free', I would be lucky to snatch a sandwich around 10 p.m. before crawling into bed by 'lights out' at 11 p.m. Often I would have to tumble out of bed again as someone had forgotten to switch off the light or fallen asleep reading in bed. This meant that the generator was thundering away for just one electric light bulb — a frequent occurrence that later was to land us with the huge expense of buying another generator. Babs was with me to share the burden most summer weekends and for the school holidays but the rest of the long summers I soldiered on alone. Babs, too, was not getting the breaks she needed and had the added burden at the end of her busy term-time day of buying supplies not just for me but for our large family of helpers and the day visitors. About this time inflation began to take the bit between its teeth and the cost of food rose astronomically.

'Why are we doing this?' we asked ourselves, for we were now having to use our own income to keep the island open to visitors and to feed the helpers. We had no time to enjoy the island in the lovely summer months and were getting exhausted into the bargain. However it seemed such a worthwhile project and appreciated by so many. 'The highlight of our holiday' was, and is, a constant refrain. We were, too, able to show young people a way of life that was fast disappearing and introduce them to old crafts that were new to them, for at that time there had not been the resurgence of interest in crafts that there is today.

It was not all one-sided either. Many did fine work and we remember them over the years. Such a one was Julian. A shy graduate, he was a most willing worker and when there was a wearisome job to be done he would volunteer. With so many people living on the island during the summer, water was a precious commodity. To conserve it for drinking and cooking, sea-water had to be hauled up to flush the lavatories. Every morning, or when the tide was high enough, the helpers had to bring up buckets of sea-water from below the jetty to fill a tank for the outside lavatory used by themselves and day visitors. This was an irksome and a tiring and unpopular task. Some helpers would be missing at the vital time; not so Julian — he was always there and toiled unceasingly with buckets full to the brim in either hand.

Always after they left the island helpers wrote us letters of appreciation and thanks for the time they had spent here and the experiences and pleasure they had enjoyed. When Julian wrote he enclosed a cheque for £100 to help us with our project. This, of course, was worth much more than it is today, but it would be a sizeable sum at any time, especially when you consider that it was from a young man just starting out on his career. We decided that its most fitting use was to put it towards a system for pumping up sea-water. This we did, and now, during the summer months it is pumped, at high tide, to a tank by the outside lavatory and to another tank in the Jetty Cottage attic, thus enabling the low-flush lavatory to function without using the spring water. Of course the plumbing had to be adapted to take sea-water, and the initial cost was well in excess of £1000, but apart from cutting out the time- and energy-consuming chore of hauling it up by hand, it made life easier for summer visitors to Jetty Cottage. The pump is sited on rocks above the jetty and is dismantled for the winter; otherwise it is in danger of being swept away by storms. Once an unseasonally fierce autumn gale did just that. The tremendous seas swept over the rocks and wrenched the heavy pump from its housing, to which it was bolted, and hurled it into the surf below. As I was on the island alone I had to go down at low tide and had the back-aching task of dragging it inch by inch over the sea-bed and rocks to the bottom of the steps leading up the slope to the

path above. It was a difficult job to manhandle it up these
concrete steps for they were open and almost perpendicular.
This was followed by a long and slow drag up the steep slope to
safety. So now, at the end of the summer when the last visitor or
helper has departed, we make sure that it is dismantled and
stored away until the following season, for there is plenty of
spring water for our own needs. However, as far as we are
concerned it will always be 'Julian's pump', and he certainly has
done his bit for the island.

In spite of help and encouragement such as this the strain was
becoming unendurable. With hindsight it seems incredible
that we carried on like this for so many years. One solution, of
course, was to close the island to visitors.

There was one aspect however that held us back. It was the
question of Leonard Pengelly. Although several boatmen
brought visitors to the island he was the chief ferryman. A fine
character, he was Father of the Council, for he had served on it
for thirty-five years, and a picture graced his sitting-room
showing him resplendent with the chain of office when he was
Chairman of the Council. He had given up fishing and other
trips to bring visitors to the island. He had taken us under his
wing, too, giving us fatherly advice, for he reckoned that we
were a bit green where people were concerned. 'People will
always please themselves, so you must look after your own
interests,' was something he was always preaching to us,
wagging his finger, and looking at us with his keen blue eyes.
Over the years he became a very good friend to us, looked after
our interests, and helped us in many ways without thought of
reward. Once in mid-winter, when I had an abscess on a tooth,
he came over in a near gale to take me to the dentist, waited for
me and brought me back, carefully wrapping a scarf round my
face. He would accept no payment. 'I was glad to be of help,' he
said. Although getting on for seventy he was still a fine-looking
man and a great favourite with the visitors who loved listening
to his salty tales. We often think of his advice for eventually,
due to increasing age and ill health, he had to give up and sadly
he is with us no more. Highly thought of in the community, a

memorial seat was installed in his honour and memory by the entrance to the harbour.

While he was still active, however, we felt impelled to carry on; we did not feel that we should do anything that might endanger his livelihood. Then two events happened that brought things to a head. In 1973 I was commissioned to write a book and Leonard announced that at the end of the summer season he would retire, for he was already finding the handling of his boat a physical strain. Meantime the effort of writing a book, in addition to dealing with the vagaries of students' appetites, meeting visitors, catering, coping with cottagers, working in the greenhouse and cultivating the land as well as looking after myself and the pets, began to take its toll. But with Leonard retiring the solution was simple. We wrote to the Town Clerk to say that we should not be opening the following season, because, as the *Looe Guide* mentioned that the island was open to visitors, we thought that our decision should be made known officially.

For a time we revelled in the thoughts of our idyllic life to come. We should have leisure to enjoy the delights of an island summer and I would have lunch-times free from interruptions. I can truthfully say that for the whole twelve years before Babs retired from teaching I only ever had stand-up lunches during all those summers and an evening meal was a luxury to look forward to in the winter months. No wonder, in spite of a hectically active and strenuous life, I put on weight, existing as I did on an almost unvarying sustenance of sandwiches!

It was not to be. Another dream faded into never-never land. First we had a letter from the Council asking if we would reconsider our decision, as our opening the island to visitors was an added amenity for Looe. We knew this to be so, for every year visitors told us, as they do to this day, that they were spending their holiday in Looe especially so that they could visit the island. They come from far and wide, not only from all parts of the British Isles but from all over the world. They write to us from Australia, Vancouver, the United States, South Africa, the Middle East and many other places to say that they are including

Looe in their itinerary so that they can visit us. When we received the Council's letter we were glad to know that our project was appreciated and were happy to help Looe in this way, for it is a charming, picturesque fishing port and many of its inhabitants have been very good friends to us indeed.

One of these, of course, was Leonard Pengelly. He somehow got to hear about our decision to close the island and informed us that he had changed his mind about retiring; his grandson, Tony Pengelly, was going to help him. Eventually he passed on the reins to the good-looking Tony, who, with his attractive personality, was also a great favourite with visitors. When finally he took over he carried on in the tradition of his grandfather and became a good friend to us and the island. His tale will come later, for this is basically about our early days and how our life here has evolved.

We felt in view of these factors that we should carry on, at least until Leonard retired, for at that time we did not know that Tony would eventually take over from him. We are sure that Leonard, like so many locals who were born and bred in Looe, loved the island and wanted us to carry on, as, so we were touched to hear, it was thought that 'we were good for the island'. But how to carry on? We had been told that we were eligible for grants for projects such as ours, but we did not favour this on two counts. Firstly, there would possibly be strings attached and we should no longer be free agents; secondly we did not believe in grants. We felt, and still do, that it is up to us to make a success of our projects. Physical help, gifts and donations freely given was one matter, a spur to our endeavours and the greatest encouragement we could have; but expecting grants as of right was another and not in our reckoning.

At last after much pondering we emerged through this labyrinth of thorny problems with a change of direction that we hoped would prove a solution, albeit a compromise. We would offer self-catering working holidays, and make a nominal charge for accommodation. Secretly I hoped that this would discourage volunteers from applying. Without helpers there could be no visitors and, *ipso facto*, freedom and solvency would be ours again.

To this end we advertised our working holidays in *The Lady* and elsewhere, as well as sending notices to *The Conserver* and the National Union of Students. The response amazed us, for not only did the applications increase but they came from people of all ages and backgrounds — professional couples with young families, others with teenage offspring. They were glad, they told us, to escape from the rat race for a while, help in a worthwhile project and give their children a holiday in natural surroundings that would encourage them to join in communal projects. Surprisngly we had applications from OAPs too, and these have proved to be among our most enduring helpers, returning year after year. These veterans were young or in their prime during the war and as such have thrown off the image of grannies in shawls or bent old gentlemen. Leading active and often dangerous lives in those historic times they are forever forward-looking and have a resilience and a 'Give us the tools and we will get on with the job' outlook that puts many younger people to shame. Sally Roberts is one of these. She skis and partakes in many active pursuits, yet finds the time and energy to come here, often twice a year, from near Liverpool, with her friend Clare Donnelly, to help us at our busiest times on the land; and Margery Roberts (but no relation), who comes especially to help us with jam-making. A book could be written about our helpers — and probably will — for they are part of the fabric of our lives here, in the spring and summer. Young and old become a good 'mix' and everyone seems to enjoy living and working with others from differing backgrounds, and many friendships have been formed.

At the time this new *modus operandi* eased the burden to some extent and enabled me to carry on while Babs lived for the most part on the mainland, especially as cottagers joined in and helped also. But I longed for the day when Babs could retire and join me. TV programmes and articles in the National Press about our activities brought us to the public notice and more and more people came to see us. There were now up to five boatmen ferrying visitors to the island. One occasion I remember in particular, early in the season, when there were no helpers. Simultaneously five boats arrived, two disgorging visitors at the jetty and three on the beach. I had to race up the path and along the cliff top and back like a demented being to meet them. Sometimes the numbers involved were few but the mechanics of helping them off the boats, catering to their needs and helping them on the boats again were the same. Sometimes in fine weather there would be a great influx and with more good weather predicted, I would, after a hectic day, stay up half the night baking scones. Unexpectedly a gale would blow up or the wind turn easterly and prevent boats leaving the harbour for days on end. With no deep-freeze facilities, trays and trays of scones and a stock of bread bought in anticipation would all go mouldy and the expensive clotted cream go off.

Sometimes, without warning, the weather broke in early September and, with the visitor season coming to an abrupt and unexpected end, we were left with large quantities of foodstuff that would not over-winter in our damp sea atmosphere. Coffee congealed, sugar and flour hardened, tea turned mouldy, butter went rancid and tins rusted. It was no wonder that the National Trust official said that opening the island to visitors was not a viable proposition.

It never has been. With rising costs Babs and I have had to dig deeper and deeper into our own pockets to provide and maintain accommodation and facilities for visitors and helpers, with, of course, the added and increasing cost of transport of goods and labour from the mainland. Often we are still tempted to close the island and revert to the help of friends and the offers of voluntary organizations for the conservation and cultivation of the island which is our primary aim. We dream often of a more leisurely life, when in summer we could go on cliff walks, have picnics on the beach, swim in the heat of a summer afternoon, have lunch-times *sitting down*, free from interruptions, and we could at last be able to achieve the simple but impossible delight of sitting on top of the island in summer-time to enjoy the view and the peace — just like our visitors.

There are moments when we do not think our efforts are worth the strain on our energy and finances; then along will come someone whose encouragement will put us on course again. One such is Kath Barker who regularly, sometimes twice a year, makes the long journey from Darlington via Dover, where she leaves her dog with her father, so that she can help us. She not only works with a will at everything, but brings some of her delicious home-baking and entertains us to delightful meals. Another such is Philla. Starting as a day visitor, she was fired by the island and our projects. She then rented a cottage, and stayed here many times with her friend, Jane, and her husband, the Rector of Botley, and their children, all of whom helped. Philla also came by herself from her busy job as a Supervisor in the Foreign Telephone Exchange in London, to stay for awhile to work on the land or do any other jobs that came to hand. Always she came with a gift, usually a bottle of malt whisky, so that, she said, we could have a 'wee dram' to cheer us along. She entertained us to many meals in the cottage and over the years has proved to be a most generous friend. Eventually she retired and moved from London to Liskeard so that she could be within easy reach of the island.

A recent ploy of hers was to arrange an official birthday for me. Babs's birthday is in June, a time of year when there is an island population. Consequently she has cards or presents from all who are here; the St George's flag is flown and a birthday party arranged. Mine is in late October, a time of gales, no visitors, and too rough for the flag to be hoisted anyway. Indeed until Babs retired I often spent it alone, celebrating at a weekend when it was calm enough for her to come over for a few hours. Philla always sends me a present, but that is not good enough for her — she likes to give it in person.

Independence Day, 4 July, was fixed, as it was already the date designated for the birthday of Lucky, the terrier-cum-labrador successor to Kim, and that of Tilly and Samantha, two of the cats who had eventually replaced Cleo, HamRam and Bessie. Their exact birthdays were not known but they were within a week or two of this date. Sue, the youngest cat, who now looks after me in place of Joan, has a known birthday, as does Emma our other dog — a Christmas present to Lucky from Sue, the vet, who until she left the district, undertook the welfare of all our pets, and in the process became an island addict. All the pets were invited to a party and the flag was hoisted. Pam Burdass, who was helping indefatigably in many ways, baked a cake as a surprise. A good time was had by all except that the cats decided not to show up — they were not party minded, they said. The dogs had a wonderful time and I basked in the glory of an official birthday — just like the Queen. Typically Philla sent me another present on my real birthday, so now I have two birthdays, but without, I hope, a corresponding increase in age. Others got to hear about this and sent me 'royal' birthday card greetings and Paul and Sandra Hughes sent me a beautiful book on wild flowers, illustrated by Marjorie Blamey, the artist, who lives in Liskeard.

We first met Paul when he came as a day visitor when he was a schoolboy of fourteen. He was remembered in particular because he dashed back to the mainland by the return boat to fetch a scientific journal dealing with the habits of seagulls we had been discussing with him. He was keenly interested in zoology and this became his specialist subject. Later he came here on working holidays and we learned from him many fascinating facts about the numerous seaweeds that grow around our shores. He kept in touch during his university days, once paying us a flying visit to give us a beautifully illustrated book on insects which has proved invaluable in our study of the wealth of wildlife to be found on the island. His sister, Clare, came on working holidays, too, and has now completed her training as an actress. Paul, now qualified and launched on his career in a hospital, brought his girl-friend, Sandra, on a working holiday, in the hope that the island would mean as much to her as it did to him. Fortunately she fell under the spell of the island too, and we were very happy to welcome them back here for their honeymoon.

Jane Cochrane, now a radiographer, was another who started as a schoolgirl helper. She met Andrew Giles here who had recently left school. Their friendship blossomed and each year they came on a working holiday together and last March (1984) they married, spending a day of their honeymoon with us.

Many of our student helpers whose careers have taken them far afield have never forgotten their time here; they keep in touch and bring us up to date with their progress. Sarah Kelly, who started as a schoolgirl helper, now a doctor and training to become a surgeon, writes to us regularly and still comes to help when she can find time in her busy life, with her brother Adam, originally a schoolboy helper and now a falconer. There is one who went to Alaska and after nine years, on a visit to this country, came to see us and asked if she could stay overnight so that she could show us her photographs and dig a patch for us. This she did and, forever, this area is dubbed the 'Alaska Patch'. Another was Pat Nevin, who after she had qualified took a medical research job in Hawaii. She sends us a colourful calendar from there every year and, when she came on a flying visit to this country for the Royal Wedding, came to see us and brought us a coral necklace apiece from her adopted island. Carol Alvin, who was on a sponsored cycle ride for the National Trust of Scotland round the coast of Britain, gave up a week of her time to help us and now lives on an island herself — the Isle of Coll. She writes interestingly to us of her life and has had several articles published about her island activities.

These and many more are interwoven in the pattern of our lives here: the families, the OAPs, the young men and women — the older ones too, who come year after year to help, bearing gifts for the island or for us personally. Many have thrown parties for us or invited us to meals. This year two young students, who were here at the end of the season, Debbie and Jacque, invited us to a candle-lit three-course gourmet meal.

We feel that all these special people deserve that we respond to their encouragement and friendship. In our darker moments, when we are tempted to close and lead a more leisurely life in the tranquil days of summer, we remember them and others who have inspired us. Such a one was Michael Trinick, the Regional Director of the National Trust, who visited us in 1982 before his retirement and said that the National Trust depended on private owners such as ourselves, who are willing to open their property to the public and preserve it on National Trust lines, an uneconomic undertaking beyond the resources of the Trust. After his visit Michael Trinick wrote us a letter in which he said; 'I was very taken with the relaxed atmosphere you had created there, and felt you must give much pleasure to many people.'

Such sentiments sustain us and enable us to carry on, and so we shall — as long as the money lasts.

The **COTTAGERS'** *Tale*

During the early period when I was alone on the island, out of the blue came a letter from the Bahamas. It was from a First Secretary who had read an article of mine in a magazine in his Embassy. He said that he was coming on home leave and would like to rent the Smugglers' Cottage if that were possible. This did not appeal to me at all. We were not established ourselves and were still having many problems, especially with the pumping of the fresh water, and, as it was term time, I should be here alone. I did not think that I would be up to coping with a First Secretary. 'He will be too high-powered for me,' I wailed to Babs. 'From an Embassy! He will be used to cocktail parties — formal dinners — just like the Navy, all gold braid and protocol. He won't be able to stand it here.' I tried to put him off. 'Primitive compared with the mainland,' I said. 'Water problems.' Nothing would deter him. The correspondence went on for some time. 'I am coming,' he said, 'if you will have me.'

So he and his wife came; his daughter could not as it was term-time and she would still be at school — Roedean. All my fears were groundless. 'You mentioned the water situation,' he said, 'I have spent all my life abroad and we have always had to *buy* our water. I shall be happy to help you in any way,' he added. And help he did. Stripped to the waist he toiled on the land; he carted stores in the caterpillar tractor, and he heaved coal up from the beach. In particular he took over tending the freshwater pump in the cliff. At this stage in its life it had an unpleasant habit of coming apart at the seams when the engine was started, drenching whoever was there with cascades of icy spring-water. As this was usually Babs or me we were delighted that our diplomat added this to the chores that he undertook. Not only did he enjoy his holiday, possibly as a refreshing change from the diplomatic rounds, but we certainly enjoyed having him and we were sorry when his leave was up and he left for Romania.

Later on when we were established and let the cottages occasionally during the summer months, there was one booking Babs made that for a similar reason caused me much nail-biting. It was for a Colonel, whose home was a Manor House. 'Not the Army!' I wailed to Babs. I always seemed to moan if any bookings were made although I knew these were necessary to keep the cottages 'alive'. 'He will be snooty, élitist. Not for us!' Now that we were settled into island life we lived in jeans, gumboots, fisherman's smocks, anoraks and woolly hats; they had become *de rigueur*. We had cast off the clothes and trimmings of civilization like a chrysalis — not to emerge as butterflies, but more like your bucolic peasant. I really enjoyed being a peasant, and the prospect of coming face to face with a senior officer in the Army appalled me. We couldn't be so lucky as with the First Secretary. 'Well,' said Babs, 'it's too late. I have booked him,' and hoofed it back to the mainland, before I could start chanting my 'Close the Island' theme.

Worse was to follow. Babs broke the news to me the following weekend, fortifying me first with a strong drink. 'He has sent his deposit,' she said, 'and he is now a Brigadier.' I spilt the drink. 'It is term-time too,' I gulped, 'I shall have to cope alone.' 'I shall be there the weekend he and his wife arrive, so keep going until I come,' said Babs.

The day he was due I was in a turmoil anyway as the electricity had become faulty and we were to have some re-wiring done. I did not have time to don my best fisherman's smock and had on my old gardening one which would not have passed any inspection nor have been fit for a collection for Oxfam.

Then I saw him. A tall distinguished man with grey hair. He stood languidly at the top of the path, hand on hip, watching a short, stocky man beavering up the path. Glistening with perspiration he was pushing with all his might and main the truck piled high with baggage. 'Good God!' I cried, 'he has even brought his batman with him.' The Brigadier did not attempt to help — well, he wouldn't, would he? At last the stocky man and his caravan of luggage made the top of the path, turned and disappeared into the Jetty Cottage entrance. Shortly after this Babs arrived. 'He's brought his batman with him,' I hissed. 'I didn't see any batman. I met him on the quayside — he is an awfully nice man,' said Babs cheerfully. 'Come and be introduced.' Down we went to the cottage and I found myself shaking hands with the stocky one, only he was not stocky any more now that he was no longer bent double from labouring up the path with the truckload of luggage.

'Who, then', I asked Babs back at the house, 'was that tall distinguished man watching at the top of the path?' 'Oh! him', said Babs. 'That would be Mike the electrician. I am so glad that he could get over today.'

During their stay the Brigadier's wife asked me about a piece of kitchen equipment that was new to her. 'That is a steamer,' I replied. 'Babs bought it in France. I am not sure how to use it myself — it's a bit different from ours. I will ask her on the radio telephone.' That night I told Babs that the Brigadier's wife was having trouble with the French steamer, and could she help? The line was crackling a bit and I had to repeat what I had said. Babs sounded really concerned. 'I will ring up the coastguard,' she said. 'I shouldn't have thought that was necessary,' I said. Babs knew him quite well but I had never heard that he was a great one in the culinary arts. 'And why should he know anyway?' I asked. 'Well,' shouted Babs above the crackling 'if it's a French steamer of course he should. What makes you so sure it is French?' 'You bought it in France, so you should know,' I yelled back. By the time we had reconciled Babs buying up part of the French Merchant Navy in trouble on the high seas with a piece of kitchen equipment that was perplexing a Brigadier's wife we did not know which sounded louder, the crackling of the atmospherics or our hysterics.

He was not the only one we suspected would be too grand for

us and our simple existence but who slipped into island life like
a glove. Another was a director of a prestigious firm of Saville
Row tailors who had booked the Jetty Cottage for himself and
his family for a month. During his holiday nothing gave him
greater pleasure than to scrape down and paint boats for us. He
did this year after year, asking us to make sure there would be a
boat for him to paint the following year. He travelled
world-wide in the course of his business and he said that
painting boats and living the simple life in beautiful, tranquil
surroundings was wonderful therapy after the pressures of his
life. He added that it was a privilege to help and thanked us for
allowing him and his family to share our island with them.

We have found surprisingly that the highly successful,
hard-working business men who come here seem to find their
greatest relaxation, not in sitting on a beach soaking up the sun,
but by channelling their energies into some useful physical
pursuit that does not tax their brains unduly. It gives them a
feeling of achievement with a tangible end-result without the
harassment of schedules, responsibilities, the demands of
people, telephones and so on. We have found so often that these
well-heeled city gents enjoy the contrast to their highly
pressurized lives. We are not quite sure about their wives, who
cannot shed the burden of cooking and housekeeping, but
dutifully they adapt so that their husbands may for a while
relax, the peace of the island acting as a balm to soothe their
overwrought nerves.

One cannot, however, make hard and fast rules; we could not
expect that all business men, like this director, would find their
Elysium here. We therefore viewed with some apprehension one
applicant for the Jetty Cottage. Roger Mitchell apparently
owned his own firm in London, and the correspondence was
conducted by his private secretary. Our concern deepened when
the secretary wrote saying that having dealt with all the
correspondence she would love to come herself on holiday and
could she book the Smugglers' Cottage for herself and her boy
friend? As this was for a date prior to her boss's booking we

could not help but suspect that she had been sent to 'case the joint' and find out if it were up to his standards.

The secretary and the boy friend duly arrived and were installed in the cottage. It was early in the season, not too early for day visitors but we had not so far established a regular supply of voluntary helpers, and student helpers were not yet free. I was, therefore, having to do everything alone. As it was an exceptionally low spring tide I had to trundle two heavy trolleys and several planks far out into the Island Roads to take the visitors off the boats. I then accompanied them up the path where I gave them a welcoming chat by the house, and so on to serving teas and refreshments. In between I had to wash up as we had not yet acquired enough crockery to run through more than one or two sets of visitors without doing so. On departure the visitors had to be helped on to the boats again. With everyone coming and going at intervals and as the trolleys and planks had to be dragged up as the tide came in I was hard put to keep everything going smoothly. Most cottage people love to help as we had already found and usually they would happily see visitors on and off the boats and take charge of the trolleys. Not so our secretary and her friend, and for three days I did not even see them. I could only assume that they were indeed reconnoitring for the boss, or that perhaps they did not know what was going on and, like others, it was taking time for them to adjust.

On the third day, exhausted as I was from the constant racing up and down the path, numbering some twenty times, the trundling of the heavy trolleys, all the café work, but, most of all, the talking to visitors, I just flopped down in the kitchen at the end of the day, too tired even to think about a meal. There was a knock on the door. I opened it. There stood the boy friend, with a bucket in his hand and there beside him was the secretary with a bottle of whisky in hers. 'We think you need some help,' they said. 'We have come to clean your windows, and would you like a drink?' Bless their hearts! they set to and cleaned all the spray-driven windows which I had not even noticed, I was so used to the house being constantly buffeted by storms. We all

had drinks. Then they invited me down to the cottage for a
meal. We had a rollicking time. From then on they helped me
in every way and I was constantly invited to meals. We had
musical evenings too. I put on for them a particularly fine
recording of Beethoven's Violin Concerto. Not only that, we
had live performances, too, for the boy friend was a musician
and had brought his violin with him. The secretary seemed to
have an unlimited supply of whisky and I soon found no
difficulty at all in wagging my finger at her and saying: 'Do you
know, Babs and I thought that you had been sent here as a spy!'
She looked nonplussed, as well she might, for dealing with the
correspondence had merely whetted her appetite for a holiday on
the island herself.

One day she went ashore for reinforcements and came back
full of excitement. 'There is a harmonium for sale in a little
antique shop in West Looe,' she said. 'Let's go and buy it,' I
cried instantly, for Babs was with us now and some helpers had
arrived. We were off on the next boat — on to the quayside and
into the shop before someone else snapped it up. 'How much is
the harmonium?' I asked. 'It's not a harmonium, it's an organ
and it is twenty,' the antique dealer replied. 'Twenty what?' I
quavered. Did he meant twenty grand — an organ could surely
command a princely sum. 'Twenty pounds,' he said. 'I'll have
it!' I snapped. If Babs and I could buy an island in ten seconds
flat, an organ was a mere tit-bit, and who would not buy an
organ at £20? Certainly not the two of us, for I knew that Babs
would be in complete agreement. Usually we only disagreed
over something unimportant such as whether we needed a fresh
'J' cloth or if it would do for one more day, or some such
triviality; never about anything so important as an island or an
organ. 'What is more,' added the dealer, 'I will help get it over
to the island.' He told us about its history. It was in fact an
American organ some 100 years old and one of a type popular at
the time in village churches throughout Cornwall. This
particular one was from Talland church a few miles down the
coast, and was being replaced by an electric one. This excited
Babs and me beyond measure. According to the sketchy history

we had been able to trace about the island it had been
established that the church at Talland was the parent church for
the island chapel, whose earliest recorded date was 1139 —
although it was thought that it may have dated back to even
earlier times. Both the island chapel and the church at Talland
came under the See of Glastonbury. That the Talland church
organ was now to come to the island seemed just part of this
mysterious power that we felt had guided us here too.

Getting the organ over to the island — that was the problem.
In the end about six men volunteered to take part in the
operation. There was the antique dealer; Bob Whitewood, a big
muscular friend of ours; Jack Tambling, a stalwart Cornishman;
the violinist and a couple of extras picked up from the quayside.
Without the use of a crane or even a hoist, but with much
ingenuity and a great deal of brawn, they managed to
manhandle it from the quayside into the open motor-boat.
With the six men and Babs, the organ now made its historic
journey over to the island. On arrival it was even more difficult
to heave it upwards out of the bucking boat and on to the jetty.
Having negotiated the steps and the paths to the house, further
problems faced them. They managed to manoeuvre it along the
hall although this presented difficulties, for, wide as the hall is,
there was little enough room for the organ and six men around
it. It was when they reached the end and had to turn into the
non-U lounge that it seemed impossible; that was, until they
ripped off a cabinet that was fixed to the wall at the end of the
hall. At last the perspiring men, after removing a large
bookcase, managed to position it in place and in no time at all
the organ was installed, the bookcase shunted up the stairs to a
bedroom and the cabinet refixed to the wall. Over drinks all
round everyone felt that the day had been crowned with success,
and in addition we had started to extend our library upstairs.

This is not the end of the organ saga, but for the time being it
must be left to settle itself into its new environment for soon it
would be time for Roger Mitchell and his family to arrive.

On his first day he came up to me in the courtyard by the
tractor shed where I was sorting out the latest boatload of stores.

'Is there anything I can do to help?' he asked. 'You could help move some of these up to the house,' I answered, trying not to sound too eager. 'Of course,' he replied, 'but I meant generally — I understand it is usual to help.' 'What do you like doing?' I asked speculatively, ('Admin' pricking up its ears — get the right man for the right job and you are made). 'Well,' he said, 'I wondered about a bit of track clearing, perhaps.'

So to this very day we have a track called 'Roger's Way', for he spent the whole of his fortnight's holiday cutting, chopping and hacking swathes through the bramble to form a new track where perhaps no man had trod for centuries. It went round the outer perimeter of the southern cliffs down to High Cove on the rocky western seaboard. By the end of his holiday a car could have been driven there, it was so wide and clear. Unfortunately it becomes overgrown every year, for with the mild climate we enjoy, unhindered by frost, everything burgeons into lush growth from early spring. However, Roger led the way and each year helpers find traces of his track and clear it once again.

The first evening he invited me down to the cottage for drinks. There, to my unaccustomed eyes, was a vast array of gin, vodka, whisky and sherry — just like the cocktail parties of old. 'What would you like?' he asked. 'Gin and tonic, please.' This was the pinnacle of sophistication indeed after my homely if delectable fare of home-made wine. He looked disappointed. 'Haven't you any?' I inquired politely. 'It is not that,' he said, 'but I understood from my secretary that your taste is for whisky.' How was he to know that I go along with the adage 'When in Rome . . . .' His secretary's tipple was whisky and so, during her stay, it was mine. Similarly, when I was in the WRNS I joined my naval friends in a diet of pink gin or rum according to their rank. I am sure that if a Russian were to turn up here with a firkin of vodka I would soon give the impression that vodka was the only drink for me. Babs arrived for the summer holidays and all the time during their stay we were both invited to evening drinks with Roger and Averil, and a very welcome break it made for us.

Living on the job we are never away from its endless demands, summer or winter. In the summer season the pressure is tremendous — to have lunch without interruptions, constant knocks on the door, calls from the field telephone on the beach and visitors needing to be met, is a luxury never to be enjoyed for months at a time. To prepare an evening meal and eat it before 10 o'clock at night is an almost impossible dream and so often it has to be the inevitable sandwich, for cottagers, helpers and pets with their unavoidable requirements, plus making up the day's accounts, the baking and the washing-up, eat into the evening. The greenhouse and the land wait for no man, so digging, composting, hoeing, sowing, harvesting and making the produce thereof goes on relentlessly. Unlike people on the mainland, we can never visit friends for tea or a meal, or have an evening out with them, although we can and do entertain them here. We cannot take holidays, and a meal ashore in a restaurant — our only 'holiday' to be enjoyed once or perhaps twice in a year — needs a great deal of planning and organization to ensure that there are experienced helpers on the island to look after it, and tide and weather have to be taken into account too.

It would ease the burden for ourselves if we were to employ staff; we would need to commercialize the island to do so, but ours is a labour of love. To keep the island unspoilt and uncommercialized — a rarity these days — *and* let others share it means a great deal of sacrifice on our part and a drain on our resources and energy. We sometimes long for the early days when we lived here privately and were therefore financially self-sufficient, but so many would be the losers. Perhaps we are taking on too colossal a task in trying in our small way to stem the tide of commercialism. Nevertheless we have always been acutely aware that money is only a substitute for barter and what we have to offer is a way of life that money itself cannot buy. To keep going on these lines takes its toll and, by the end of the season, one can become exhausted mentally, physically, emotionally — and financially.

Many realize this and others, as well as Roger and Averil, invite us to drinks or a meal. Bea and John Harrington and their daughter Ann and, later, her husband especially appreciated our efforts and the strains we felt. Although a busy housewife and mother with a job in a library Bea, who surely needed a break herself, regularly invited us down to the cottage for delicious meals accompanied with wine. Bea probably never knew just how much good this did for our flagging spirits and how much enjoyment we derived from the entertaining company and good food. The whole family helped, too, in many ways, and John with his special expertise was one of the founder-members of our communications network, as is related later.

It always seems to be the busiest folk who help us the most. The Rector of Botley, Colin Wheatley, his wife Jane, accompanied by various members of their family of seven children rented the Jetty Cottage for many years. They all worked with a will to help us in many ways — on the land, in the greenhouse, and with all forms of maintenance and decorating. Jane without fail invited us down for delectable meals, and surely there can be nobody busier than a parson's wife who is also the mother of seven youngsters. Self-catering could be no real holiday for her. Philla, who appears in many of these tales, introduced the Wheatleys to the island in the first place, and always accompanied them on their holidays here. She always brought her own contributions to the feasts, often entertained us herself and never failed to present us with a bottle of whisky or some other goodie on her arrival on the island.

It is good folk like these who sustain us in our endeavours.

One of our most helpful and enduring families were the Grimers. A colleague of Babs at school, John Grimer, had a brother Peter in London, who, with his family, spent a month's holiday every summer with John at East Cliff above Looe. One day during the school holidays they all came over to see us on a day visit. Peter immediately booked a week of his month's holiday of the following year to stay with us in Jetty Cottage. He was by profession a dentist, but had, probably as an antidote, a quite fanatical interest in other pursuits, chief of which appeared to be electronics. The island was immediately added to his enthusiasms. One could say that it almost became a way of life with him. Later he had a poster about the island mounted in his sitting-room and, as a treat, every Sunday tea-time was devoted exclusively to Island talk. The highlight of their year, Peter said, was when holiday-time came round and they could once again set foot on the island of their dreams.

During the year Peter thought up all manner of ways in which he could contribute to our projects and life here. He would come armed with some item of his invention which would ease our lives or advance our projects. The first year he brought with him, among other things, some black compound used in the process of making moulds for false teeth; he thought we might find a use for it in our crafts. He also presented us with a telescope which he proceeded to mount for us at a strategic point so that one could see a wide sweep of the mainland coastline from Looe to Prawle Point in Devon in one direction, and past Eddystone Lighthouse in the other, westward towards the Lizard. Points of interest were inscribed on its stone mount and beside this we have a large RNLI lifeboat collecting-box on davits and a goodly sum is donated each year.

In discussing our plans we happened to mention that we needed some kind of communication with the beach so that helpers could tell us if any visitors had landed. Peter's eyes lighted up as he said: 'Could you possibly wait until next year? I would love to fix something for you.' It was better than waiting for ever, for at that time it was one of those fanciful pipe dreams as far as we were concerned.

Peter booked in for a fortnight for the following year. They travelled overnight by train from London and were out here by 9 a.m. As Peter stepped up out of the boat on to the jetty he called 'Have you a drill and a hammer?' Before the boat had pulled away, Peter, festooned with a coil of wire, was off down the path. By the end of the day we had 'Lift Off', for incredibly we were able to talk from the house to the beach. What Peter had installed was a field-telephone; he had hunted around for months and had at last located two ex-army instruments, which, though probably of First World War vintage, actually worked. To those brought up in the space age and used to the sophistication of electronic devices these would have been museum pieces, and our system antiquated; but to the monks of old who lived here it would have been an innovation inspired by higher powers, and thus it seemed to us. To call the beach or vice versa one cranked a handle and, powered by a bicycle lamp battery, the set at the other end would ring.

It took Peter most of his holiday to perfect the system to his satisfaction and run some of the telephone wire through spare bits of garden hose and attach it to trees and the wall of the Smugglers' Cottage garden to protect the wire from abrasion from the onslaught of winter storms. He also proposed to have an extension to the pottery where he intended to have a switchboard so that when a third instrument could be acquired we could communicate between house, pottery and beach. But time ran out on him. 'I will leave a diagram,' he said, 'with all the bits and pieces and instructions, so that if anyone turns up who knows anything about wiring he can fix it for you, which will be better than waiting a whole year until I return.' A far-away look came into his eyes and he promptly booked three weeks for the following year.

The very next visitors to the Jetty Cottage were the Harringtons. Incredibly John could not only do the wiring for the switchboard but he did not need to read the instructions. It was no trouble to him at all for he had actually been involved in installing Radar on the Pyramids during the war. Our three-way lines of communication were working in no time at all, for the resourceful Jack Tambling (who had helped with the organ) produced, like a conjuror out of a hat, a third instrument. As these instruments were so hard to come by, the whole operation, from the wish to the finished project, seemed like a miracle to us. We have been convinced over the years that if something is desirable, the wish is strong enough and the island 'genie' agrees that it is a good thing, then something or someone will turn up to bring it about. An easy philosophy perhaps, because if we do not get what we want we can always say 'the island does not want it,' and turn our thoughts to other matters. It saves a lot of useless effort too.

Peter brought other gifts — copper tubes sealed at one end to make specimen vases and suitably engraved with the St George's emblem; the inscription being made with a dentist's drill. He also presented us with some drills which were no longer good enough for drilling his patients' teeth but he thought might be useful in our crafts. One invaluable gift he made for us was a portable lamp which is still in use to this day, or rather night. It consists of a beautifully crafted wooden framework which houses a motor-bike battery; mounted on the front of the structure is a vertical fluorescent tube some twelve inches high. By some intricate wiring and gadgetry the battery is rechargeable and so will give us constant light when required. This was a great advance on the oil lamps with which we had formerly gone to bed after we had stopped the generator by turning off the last electric light switch in the house. Good as the oil lamps were they gave off fumes and this curtailed our bedtime reading; otherwise we ran the risk of being asphyxiated or, if we had the windows open, being pestered by moths. A shiny metal handle added to its good looks and made it easily transportable and, a unique touch, a dentist's syringe had been attached by a clip, in readiness for topping up the batteries. Neatly printed on the side of the frame and on the separate dial for registering the charge, which Peter had also provided, were detailed instructions for its maintenance and names of spare parts if required. Two batteries and several solderings later it is still as effective as ever, and we always give Peter a good-night blessing for his wonderfully useful and lasting gift, which is not only an example of his thoughtfulness and inventiveness but shows a nice combination of his dental and electronic skills.

The next year he booked for four weeks and thereafter he spent his month's holiday on the island and spent perhaps a day with his brother on the mainland. 'I find it cheaper too,' he explained; 'although I pay nothing to stay with John, the incidental spending of money for fish and chips, ice-creams, etc. for the children on the mainland costs more than renting the Jetty Cottage, and', he added, 'it is a better life for them.'

He could turn his hand to many things, among which were carpentry and cement mixing — the latter probably being an antidote to the mixing of minute quantities of fillings for his patients' teeth. Whatever the reason, we had the jetty kept in a state of good repair after the winter storms had battered it, and he expertly filled other cavities in walls and steps. Peter had a knack, too, of being able to knock up benches from driftwood in no time at all and most are still in use today; one in particular graces the patio where visitors have tea and has since been carved on decoratively by a series of helpers skilled in this craft; another commands a fine view across to Rame Head and beyond to Prawle Point in Devon, from a strategic point high up the hill at the entrance to 'Roger's Way'. The whole family offered to look after the island so that we could go ashore and thus, during their visits, we were able to spend a night or two in Plymouth or Falmouth foraging for stores and enjoying our one indulgence, a meal out.

What makes Peter so special is the imagination and thoughtfulness of his contributions to the island and the fact that so many of them were for us personally to ease our lives here. He is one of those who identify us with the island, knowing that without our financial support the island would have to be commercialized to enable visitors to come here, if at all, for — as he and others are perceptive enough to realize — not all island-dwellers in a paradise such as this would forego their privacy unless it were for financial gain. He and others like him will do all in their power to help us with our endeavours, and this encourages us beyond measure.

The Grimer children enjoyed the island life, too. The youngest one, Tim, arrived for the first time in a rucksack on his·father's back. Later he graduated to riding on the back of Kim, our border collie, while his elder brothers John, Paul and his sister Zaz joined in all the island activities. Margaret, Peter's wife, was a champion swimmer and so was Zaz; the two of them managed to swim right round the island each time they came here; no mean feat, for the currents can be very strong and the distance is quite daunting.

Margaret and Zaz were not the only swimmers we have had here. One who stayed here caused quite a sensation. She was an attractive blonde, who with her small child was staying in the Smugglers' Cottage with a friend. The friend, who had children of her own, agreed to look after her child so that she could continue to study for her degree.

Probably as a relief from all the mental effort involved she decided to take a swim to the mainland. It happened to be a choppy sea; it was also spring tides when the sea can be fast with an undertow. We warned her about the currents and that it was too rough for Leonard to bring his boat out with visitors. 'Have no fear,' she said, 'I am a very strong swimmer, and I must go as I have run out of cigarettes.' So off she went cleaving her way through the surf with a plastic bag containing her clothes slung round her neck, and watched bemused by all the island residents. Half-way across we saw her resting on some rocks exposed by the outgoing tide, for all the world looking like Copenhagen's Little Mermaid. That was the last we saw of her for a very long time. We were very concerned, especially the friend with all the young brood at her feet.

Later that day a lone boat emerged from the harbour and bucked over the breaking seas towards the island. Leonard, with the most enigmatical look we had ever seen on his face, gave a lop-sided grin as he disgorged his lone passenger, now fully clothed. 'What happened?' asked the whole island population, who, all agog, had gathered on the beach. 'Well, my clothes got wet in spite of being in a plastic bag, so I went to the laundrette and dried them.' The mind boggled at the changing operation in the goldfish bowl of the laundrette! 'It was too rough to swim back so I persuaded Leonard to bring me.' Leonard, still with the lop-sided grin on his face, gave us one of his roguish winks as he turned into the rolling sea and headed for the harbour. Unperturbed, our swimmer went back to her studies; everyone else returned to their normal occupations in wonderment that anyone would have gone through all that for a packet of cigarettes.

The
MECHANIC'S
Tale

The best advice one can give to anyone thinking of living on an island is to take a course in DIY and to take with you a whole range of tools — and the knowledge of how to use them — or a handyman. Preferably all three.

We were not so equipped either practically or mentally. In our previous life there was always some expert friend or a professional at the end of a phone who would come at the drop of a hat to repair, maintain or put into effect some scheme of ours. The former would certainly come at the drop of a hat — the professionals took a little longer. Nevertheless we did not have to worry our pretty little heads about things that went wrong. I, in particular, was abysmally ignorant.

When we first came to live on the island I thought a plug was something one used to stop water running out of the bath, or an item by the media to promote a pop record or a book. Proudly I now know that it is a vital part of an engine and the like, which has a nasty habit of getting oiled up or dirty, thus preventing the machinery from starting up. Seemingly there is hardly a bit of mechanism that does not depend on it. Many has been the time when, over the years, I have watched strong men, stripped to the waist, sweat dripping from the end of their noses, pulling away at a piece of cord attached to some sullen bit of machinery that obstinately remained as dead as a drunk. Always there is a fringe of experts giving free advice from the sidelines. Diffident at first I lurked in the background behind this cream of the engineering world. Now I boldly step forward and in a throw-away voice nonchantly mutter! 'Perhaps it is the plug.' And — do you know? — it usually is. I then, like the Cheshire cat, dissolve rapidly into nothingness.

Luckily during the summer months the island attracts friends and visitors, who between them apparently have enough expert knowledge to sail the QE2 singlehanded, run the National Grid, to say nothing at being dab hands at plumbing, building and electronics, and have enough know-how to run up something like the Empire State Building or take the odd whirl into outer space. At least that is how it seems to non-technical, non-everything me. Mention that something does not work and unerringly someone steps forward and with a magic touch it purrs into action. Casually we would say 'A courtyard would fit in here very nicely,' or 'We would like a vineyard there,' and suddenly there *is* a courtyard, with exotic plants in full bloom, and there *is* an embryo vineyard, brave young plants in serried ranks blissfully basking southward to the sun.

My role, apart from that of producing exalted ideas, seems to be that of general run-around who supplies coffee, tea, home-made wine and tools. But how my education has improved! In those early days I did not even know the names of all those people, some of whom were friends of friends, who appeared miraculously out of thin air, and I certainly did not know my tools. So when Dave called out to me rather urgently, 'Alan Keyes!' I ran round the island yelling for him. 'It's OK,' said Dave some time later, looking at me rather strangely, as a last desperate 'ALAN! *ALAN*!' wafted hoarsely on the air, 'I've found them,' and he waved some bent pieces of metal under my eyes; keys which I now know, in my more mature island life, are indispensable for unlocking bits of metal which would otherwise be wedded until death did them part.

There was a friend of a friend who stepped off the boat one day who seemed to be an expert on everything. In no time at all everyone was treating this chap with great deference — as a kind of technical Guru. When, therefore, Peter with ashen face screamed from the boiler-house 'the boiler has sprung a leak, fetch Boss White — QUICKLY!' I panted to where I knew he was holding court by a defiant lawn-mower. 'Boss White!' I gasped, 'the boiler is leaking.' 'That's OK,' he said kindly, 'there's a tin on the shelf in the tool-shed.' Mesmerized I watched as he and Peter got to work with a tin of something that looked like white paste. For some reason I got the kudos for having found it so quickly. It seemed judicious therefore to say nothing and I merely smirked with quiet pride.

I was really on my mettle though when someone asked for a Stillson. Even I knew that it could not be a person. It sounded more like a cross between a cowboy's hat and a cheese. When we found that it was indispensable (how on earth had we lived for all those years without one?), and a superior kind of wrench, we bought one. We knew it was superior — it was so expensive. It has certainly proved indispensable for the generator and various pumps and pipes around the island, so when we were told we needed a smaller one as well, we gritted our teeth, financially speaking, and brought that one too. One day, no doubt, we shall have Father Bear, Mother Bear and Baby Bear.

During the summer months we have all these knowledgeable people to help us but during the winter we are on our own, and for twelve memorable winters, before Babs retired, the population of St George's Island, as one guide book put it, was 'One'; the 'One' being ignorant me. And it is during the winter months that machines fall sick, much as humans do. So I learned the hard way. . . .

One day I went down to the generator room to do the daily check and found the floor awash with oil. I slopped gingerly through it in my Wellington boots — for 'wellies' are not in my vocabulary. Mine are of sterner stuff, from the prototype that the grand old Duke himself might have charged around in at Waterloo. There, in the copper tubing that automatically fed the generator with fuel, was a hole out of which the diesel oil was bubbling merrily. I rushed outside to the 600-gallon storage tank and turned off the tap. This of course stopped the pipe from leaking but it also stopped the diesel oil from coming through, without which there could be no electricity. I remembered Boss White but he would not do; neither would Plastic Padding, nor any of the assortment of metal fillers which we had acquired. Frantically I read the small print — they all said the same: the object to be repaired must be clean and free of grease. This immaculate state was impossible to achieve. There was no way that I could penetrate the inside of the copper tubing to clean it; as well try to clean the inside of a piece of spaghetti.

Impasse! Concede defeat? Never! After all, I was wearing 'Wellington' boots; to surrender would be inconceivable. I would call Babs on the radio telephone and ask her to put my problem to Ken Newton, our engineer at the time. 'That's simple,' he said, 'tell her to cut out the piece of tubing either side of the hole, with a hack-saw. Join the two parts together with a piece of plastic tubing and fix them with a couple of Jubilee clips.' 'Jubilee clips!' I muttered. A picture of Queen Victoria flashed across my mind. 'Jubilee clips' — they sounded like excerpts from an old Anna Neagle film. Babs, who is knowledgeable about these things, carefully explained what a Jubilee clip looked like, and to my immense surprise, on rooting around the generator room, I found a couple of these metal clips. The plastic tubing was no problem. I had a length of this among my wine-making equipment. Armed with a hack-saw, which I now knew had nothing whatever to do with horses, I set about the operation. Surely this would not cut through metal. However to my surprise and delight the hack-saw went through the metal like butter and in a few minutes the offending piece of tubing with the hole in it was extracted. I felt like a surgeon. 'Harley Street, here I come!' I quipped to myself. Then my courage faltered. There, staring at me, were these two loose ends of copper tubing — dismembered — useless. If I could not join them together there would be no fuel supply, so no electricity, and there was a full gale blowing with no sign of a let-up. It was mid-winter, and no one would be able to get out for days, perhaps weeks.

Whenever there is a generator failure Babs and I say 'Queen Elizabeth I did not have electricity, nor did the smugglers on the island last century, and they managed quite happily.' However, going on the theory that what you do not have you do not miss, the reverse is also true. You *do* miss something that you have always had, especially if it runs your fridge and pumps from the bowels of the earth your one source of drinking water.

No Head of State, with his finger on the trigger could have felt more fraught than I, as desperately I tried to push the precious piece of plastic tubing on to the copper tube ends. It would not budge. Then I remembered tales of little boys with heads stuck in railings, and how butter or some such helped ease them free. I could do better than that. I had all this oil swilling round my feet — gallons of it. With some diligent massage, much heaving and shoving, not to mention a few oaths, at last the two vital bits of copper were encapsulated. Triumphantly I put my two new friends, the Jubilee clips, into place and screwed them tight. I went outside, turned on the fuel-tap, came in again, flicked on a light switch and *Lo! There was Light*. To this day several years later this, my frantic attempt at mechanical first-aid, still holds. As part of the tour of the island I proudly display this to those kind enough to take an interest and maybe admire it, for I do feel that it is perhaps the finest technical achievement of my career, if not of the age. Not that this success went to my head after the first giddy euphoria. I suspect that the only people who are impressed, apart from myself, are those who are even more ignorant than I am. The fact of the matter is that I do not have a rapport with mechanical objects, so it gives me great satisfaction when I strike up a working relationship with one of them, or in this case, it may have appealed to a latent nursing instinct to come to the rescue with some timely first-aid.

'What?' I ask, 'do *Dirty Contacts* mean to you?' When on one occasion the generator refused to start, the engineer when he examined it grunted 'Dirty Contacts!' Immediately there flashed into my mind a picture of seedy men in sleazy raincoats congregated in groups on a street corner in Soho. Not so. Like their first cousins 'Dirty Plugs' they hang about, not in Soho, but in electrical boxes and can cause the entire generator system to grind to a halt and plunge us into darkness. Mary Whitehouse may campaign, hold meetings and make speeches to do her cleaning up. I go armed with nothing more than a piece of emery paper and a quaking heart, for I am terrified of electricity — and with good reason. As a child I climbed a pillar outside a sea-front hotel, next to ours, the better to see a fancy dress dance being held inside. Unbeknown to me the pillar should have been surmounted by a large ornamental light bulb. This unfortunately was missing and, as I put my hand inside the top of the pillar to haul myself up, something 'live' gripped my fingers and it took a crowd of bystanders to pull me away. Although it was a lucky escape, at that tender age I did not know what danger I had been in. Nevertheless, since then I have always been suspicious of electricity. Well, you cannot *see* it, can you? It is not only fear of the unseen and the unknown, but the greater terror of grappling with this invisible enemy that assails one, at least this one.

I really do think that life on a desert island would be easier to cope with in some respects, than with one like ours, which is equipped for a more civilized existence and where the solitary inhabitant is expected to be capable of running a mini-power-station solo. We are fortunate that currently we have a goodly knight who will come charging over the sea to succour us, when our machinery falters or passes out, in the shape of Roy, an engineer, who, with his magic touch will make it leap into life again. During the winter months, however, storms hold up these rescue attempts, but now that Babs has joined me permanently the problem, although not resolved, is at least shared. With her superior knowledge of things mechanical she does not appear to be so daunted by these crises, unless of course, as I suspect, she is much braver than I am. There is the fact, too, that she did once go on a car maintenance course. When I reminded her of this she said: 'Why do you think I left half-way through the course?' 'Perhaps you learnt twice as fast as anyone else,' I replied, hoping that flattery would get me somewhere or at least somewhere away from machinery. In a way it has, for I have now appointed myself into the spectator role with the right to interfere. Standing on the sidelines I toss out some gem of knowledge culled from past experience, even the hoary old one of 'Could it be the plug?'

The
TREASURE-HUNTERS'
Tale

One of Peter Grimer's gifts was a metal detector that he had made for us. This was before they were generally popular and readily available, and we spent many a delightful hour under his direction looking for buried treasure. Mostly we were too busy and he would hunt for us. He never found the treasure which is supposed to be buried here but he did find many pieces of the land-mine which had been dropped on the island during the war. Lord Haw-Haw, the traitor who was later executed, broadcast on the radio from Germany that the battleship *St George* had been sunk. The 'battleship', in fact, was the island and the bomb crater is still there. Apparently all the damage that was done was to the conservatory, all the glass of which was blown out by the blast. I always hoped that one day Peter would unearth a Roman coin. Alas! all he found, apart from a number of modern coins, was a Victorian penny dated 1897. The special feature about this was that, not only was it Victoria's Jubilee year, but it had the appearance of having been freshly minted, for everything was in sharp relief and not worn flat as most Victorian pennies were when they were in circulation, prior to decimalization.

More interesting were two cannon balls which Peter found buried on the main beach. They were encrusted with rust and so misshapen that they looked almost square. When the rust was removed, however, two complete cannon balls were revealed. How they came to be on the landing-beach which faces the mainland, just a short distance across, is a mystery so far unsolved. The first confrontation with the Spanish Armada in 1588 took place a few miles due south of the island, as copies of maps of the period show. Skirmishes with the French would have taken place in this area too. Did the fleet practise off the island in the days of cannon ball, or did a shore battery shoot short of its target at sea? There is an old gun emplacement on the island facing due south, so this suggests that during an exchange of firing with the enemy there may have been an overshot from the sea. We do not know, but they are now part of our collection of flotsam and jetsam and other finds, for we hope one day to have a small maritime museum of articles found or washed up here.

Peter, in fact, was not the first to present us with a metal detector, although it was not an electronic job, more your basic dowsing outfit. One of our earliest visitors to Jetty Cottage was a technician who worked for the Gas Board. He was a friendly chap who often visited us in our kitchen to have a glass of home brew and a chat. Over one or two glasses of my best elderflower wine he revealed what to us was a startling fact. The Gas Board, he said, employed someone to go dowsing for hidden pipes. The equipment used, he added, was nothing more than two stout copper wires, bent at one end at right angles to form handles. Held by the dowser, he said, the wires crossed when they were passed over metal, and presumably water. As it so happened I had a stock of stout copper wires in my Wirecraft kit. In no time at all we were all outside to try our hand at dowsing. Although the wires would not react to everyone, they did for Babs and me. First we tested them by throwing down pieces of metal, then in case auto-suggestion played a part they were buried out of sight. To our great surprise and gratification the wires crossed every time over the buried metal. We explored untried ground and whenever the wires crossed there was always something metallic under the surface — they even reacted to silver paper hidden from view. They always worked over water, too, but as we could see this we did not think it was a reliable test.

We were not the first to try dowsing on the island, for we had been told that some years previously a professional lady dowser had been asked to locate sources of fresh water. According to our informant she had found it in abundance in various parts of the island, although whether this was before or after the tunnel had been bored into the cliff was not known.

As we had more immediate chores than looking for buried treasure we put the wires aside. Then one day a letter arrived, out of the blue, from a stranger. It was from a clergyman in Cumbria. A relative, he said, had visited our island the previous year and was most impressed with our efforts on the island. He himself was of Cornish descent. He enclosed something carefully wrapped in tissue paper, which he said had been in his family for generations. He would like us to have it. Inside the tissue paper was a yellowing piece of paper, brittle and fragile to the touch with age. It was a rough hand-made map in faded brown ink showing where treasure was buried on St Michael's Island — the former name of St George's Island. The writing and spelling were of a bygone age. We looked at it boggle-eyed. Was it a hoax? How could it be? The letter heading was that of a Priory; the writer was obviously who he said he was. Was the map genuine? Why, if it were some schoolboy prank of an earlier century, would it have been treasured for so long, and find its way to a branch of the family so remote from Cornwall as Cumbria? The clergyman went on to say that he doubted that the treasure still existed, but if we did find anything perhaps we would be good enough to let him know. He was very happy for us to have the map and he wished us well in our projects on the island.

When we first came here local folk had told us many tales of smugglers' tunnels to the mainland and buried treasure. 'The last smuggler left without revealing where the treasure was buried,' was an oft-repeated saying. Smugglers, we knew, had lived on the island. The descendants of one of the most famous, Amram Hooper, had actually been to visit us. And we do know for a fact the existence of one tunnel. Soon after our arrival one of Looe's most respected older inhabitants came to see us. He was Mr Pearn, of the well-known boat-builders of Looe of that name. At the time he was eighty-five and we felt honoured that he should make the journey to see us. The purpose of his visit, he said, was to show us where a tunnel had actually existed. He took us out to the cliff face. It had been buttressed with stonework to form a bulwark against the storms and the constant danger of erosion and landslides. In the centre of the stonework he traced with his finger the outline of a door in cement. This, he said, was the entrance to the tunnel before it was filled in with concrete. He then took us back to the room we used as a transit camp. 'This', he said, 'used to be a barn. When I was a boy of ten I used to come here picnicking with some other lads. One day we fell through the floor into a tunnel, and there are some who say that the tunnel continues up to your kitchen.' We subsequently tapped all the flagstones in the kitchen and found one that indeed sounded hollow. We have not, however, so far tried to prise it up.

The most extraordinary thing about the map now in our possession was that a tunnel was shown leading to the treasure; the entrance to it was marked with a cross, and the cross was the exact spot that Mr Pearn had pointed out to us on the cliff face. This suggested that there were two tunnels leading from the same entrance in the cliff — the one leading to the barn and the other to the treasure.

We suppose that most people on receiving such a map would have been tempted to go out immediately and start digging. We did not. Apart from having little spare time from the tasks that threatened to engulf us, we felt that it was preferable to believe that buried treasure was lying there waiting to be discovered, than to dig and perhaps find nothing and so have a romantic dream shattered. Many people would not have understood this but we did not tell them — we did not tell anybody. Partly because we were afraid that we would be invaded by an army of visitors armed with pickaxes and shovels and we would perforce have to put up a notice 'NO DIGGING FOR BURIED TREASURE'. More recently, with the advent of sometimes indiscriminate use of metal detectors, we have had to put up a notice forbidding their use. In particular we do not want the chapel site despoiled against the time when we hope to have it expertly dug by archaeologists. Another reason was that

we did not think that the last smuggler would have cared for
hordes of strangers poking around — or the monks either. For it
is our fancy that the monks might have buried some of *their*
treasure here, too, at the dissolution of the monasteries. As the
chapel came under the See of Glastonbury what more likely a
place could they find to hide their precious possessions, we
reasoned, than on this remote island. Neither the Holy Grail
nor the Golden Gate have ever been traced, so it is not too
fanciful a supposition.

We did not tell anyone about the map until five years later.

By that time we had regular voluntary helpers, one of whom,
by dint of his enthusiasm and predilection for hard work will
always be remembered. Phil Deem was a Devon boy of
nineteen. His looks belied his age for he had about him an air of
maturity and seriousness of purpose that augured well for his
future; he had already been accepted as a trainee manager with
W.H. Smith, and during the five years he came here on
working holiday he progressed up the scale until he was
promoted to the Managership of one of their large branches. As
his responsibilities grew so we saw correspondingly less of him,
but he still kept in touch as much as his busy life allowed.

One of Phil's major contributions was the digging of an
embryo reservoir. With the advent of visitors to the island the
storage of sufficient spring water against the times of summer
drought became a major problem. Abundant for our own
purposes, it had to be eked out when we had as many as twenty
people staying on the island, as well as day visitors wanting cups
of tea or coffee.

So we tossed the idea in the air that what we needed was a
reservoir; this was in case someone who knew about these
matters picked up our signal. The first one to do so was Jim, the
husband of Ivy, a friend from Epsom Art School. Jim and Ivy
Denner came to stay so that Ivy could help me with pottery, for
she was an experienced potter, who held her own exhibitions, so
her help would be invaluable to me. Jim was Managing Director
of a large industrial firm and by profession was a quantity
surveyor. We learned somewhat to our chagrin that a reservoir is

not just a hole in the ground. There were certain aspects to be considered, such as water pressure, and this and the size of the hole were interrelated — or so we understood. There was an answer to it all however; it was just a matter of calculation, Jim said, and set about doing clever things with slides rules and the like. He produced a diagram giving the exact depth, length and breadth that would hold 'X' cubic feet of water or it may have been tons, I really cannot remember. I only know that this diagram became a treasured document to be carefully stored until such time as someone picked up our next 'radar' signals, as we were pleased to call them. Phil, in his indomitable way, was on to the idea like flash. 'I will dig your reservoir,' he said, and with great enthusiasm and vigour he laid about with pickaxe and shovel, just below the storage tanks in the woods — the designated site. He spent the whole of his fortnight's holiday, hacking, digging and heaving earth. By the end of his holiday the hole was finished — an impressive twenty feet square and some six feet deep, the exact measurements required being checked and re-checked.

And there alas! it remains to this day — just a hole. To finish the job was not just a matter of expense but of expertise. However well it was lined, with concrete or other suitable material, there was the important question of the lid or covering. As the reservoir was to be an integral part of our spring-water storage system, the cover was of paramount importance. The danger of branches, twigs, emmets or even more objectionable objects floating on the surface of our drinking-water meant that it had to have a thoroughly everything-proof roof, and the solution to this has so far eluded us. Our spring water is delicious and we do not want to run the risk of even the merest touch of pollution, by the danger of invasion or infiltration by foreign bodies. No doubt at the right time some Merlin will arrive on the scene with the solution, unless of course the island, knowing that there is ample water for the two of us and our pets, does not want to run the risk of increasing the resident population.

The following year Phil arrived, no doubt expecting to find

the reservoir fully operational. To mollify him and because we felt inordinately guilty about all his efforts coming to naught, we decided to tell him about the buried treasure and that he, and he alone, should be the one to dig for it. His eyes lighted up, all thoughts of his lovely but unused pit forgotten. We swore him to secrecy, then at dead of night, some five years after receiving the map, and armed with pickaxe, shovel, map and copper wires we marched out to the spot marked 'Treasure' on the map. We held the wires out in front of us and walked slowly around the area. Suddenly the wires began to cross. There was no mistaking their reaction. Time and time again they almost bent back double for both Babs and me, and always at the same spot, marked 'X' on the map. Phil started digging. The next night after 'Lights Out' at 11 p.m. we crept out again and Phil went on digging.

By now there was a sizeable hole. During the day, so as not to excite too much curiosity, it was covered with a tarpaulin. We *think* Phil told everyone, including curious day visitors, that he was trying to locate a water pipe. However, as is the way with these affairs, the secret leaked out among those staying on the island, and every evening thereafter, when the day visitors had departed, our little island population gathered round while Phil swung and shovelled. By the end of his fortnight's holiday he was up to his neck and still the wires crossed beneath his feet. Regretfully he roughly filled in the hole, which was some six feet square, and covered it over to await his return the following year. This time his head disappeared completely from view, and he was a tall fellow. The area he now covered was extensive, too, and would have made a reservoir itself if we could have channelled water there. By the end of his holiday all we could see was a flaying axe-head, and great clods of earth hurled up to the sky. And still the wires crossed at the bottom.

But time had run out. Phil was now off into the realms of higher management which precluded any more holidays digging for buried treasure. Sorrowfully he had to fill in the enormous pit he had dug. To avoid subsidence this was done in the first place with old tins and bottles, the disposal of which is always a problem as ne'er a dustman passes our way. The top-soil was removed to the greenhouse and finally the turves were relaid. When later we re-examined the walled-up entrance to the tunnel that Mr Pearn had shown us we realized that the tunnel would have extended to well below the level Phil had reached, so if we do not initiate any more attempts to explore deeper perhaps these clues will help some future islander, who will not be so engulfed in the multifarious activities that seem to be our lot, or who may not think, as we do, that the island itself is treasure enough.

In fact this was not our very first hunt for buried treasure, and it was before we had a map to guide us. As I was not exactly there I cannot give much information about it. I say 'I was not exactly there' because it happened in a curious way. A friend of mine of long-standing, Di Sorby, and her friend Winifred Hatherly, had come from London to spend a week or so with us. This was during our very early days when we were not only putting down our roots but also branching out in several directions. This entailed a great deal of correspondence, and as Di and Winifred were experienced secretaries they offered to type our letters for us. One evening after a particularly busy session we had a get-together with one or two others who were staying to help in various ways, as a relaxation and little light relief. There was much hilarity as, over glasses of home-made wine, Babs and I regaled them with tales of our experiences in moving over to the island — the wine, of course, adding to the merriment. We also related the tales we had been told by locals of tunnels and the smugglers' buried treasure. Someone suggested that we hold a séance to find out if the spirit world would give us a message as to its whereabouts. As none of us had any claims to being a medium this idea was thankfully brushed aside.

It was then suggested that we try the wine-glass device. Cards were quickly made for each letter of the alphabet and formed in a circle on the table and a wine-glass produced and set in the centre. Then, as is usual with these affairs, there was much giggling and banter as everyone sat round the table each with a finger lightly touching the edge of the glass. Order was soon restored and the question was put: 'Would you please tell us where the treasure is buried?' There was complete silence as the glass slowly began to move. This is when 'I was no longer there' for at that precise moment I fell asleep. I did not even know that I had fallen asleep; all I do remember was waking up and finding myself sitting there completely alone — all the chairs were empty. There was just me, the wine-glass and the scattered letters of the alphabet. It was a most eerie feeling and I was greatly relieved to hear the laughter of the others returning.

Apparently the wine-glass had spelt the word 'Flagstaff', so they had all gone out with shovels and spades to the promontory where stood the flagpole near the cliff edge. But after a time their enthusiasm had waned; it was pitch dark and cold, but most of all they did not know exactly where to dig. Without an 'X' to mark the spot there was quite a large area to cover. Then there was the question of how deep? So they soon gave up trying. Also I think they all suspected each other of either consciously or unconsciously pushing the glass. Maybe, I thought, they suspected me as I was not there. But there was a strange aspect about the whole happening. The realization came to me that in the dark they had not noticed that I was not with them, or that possibly I had returned ahead of them, for when I said rather sheepishly 'I fell asleep,' someone replied, 'Yes! it *was* very tiring digging — I am off to bed.' It is for you to put what interpretation you like on the incident. I can only add that there was no more talk of digging round the flagstaff and no more sessions with the wine-glass. So far the treasure has not been found, nor indeed has it been looked for apart from these two attempts.

Is it really necessary to find it? If you live here the island is treasure trove in itself and yields riches of a material kind too. The woods and the sea provide a plentiful supply of logs and driftwood, not only for fires but for carpentry and wood carving; elderberries and blackberries, some the size of grapes, grow in profusion to give us fruit, wine, jam and other preserves; in the rock pools there are prawns, shrimps and crabs — and winkles, too, if you like them. The sea will yield a rich harvest of mullet and bass if you have time and skill enough to fish from the rocks. Nearest to the conventional concept of treasure are the semi-precious stones to be found on the shore: banded and moss agate, rose quartz and cornelian, to name a few. There is a wealth of shells, too, and sometimes even mother-of-pearl, and the many-hued pebbles, enhanced by polishing to gleam like jewels — these can all be used in our craftwork.

Perhaps the most valuable treasure is the soil. This is so fertile and the climate so unusually mild that there is seemingly no limit to the variety of crops which can be cultivated here. Grapes grow in abundance, as do figs, nectarines and peaches. Gales permitting, blackberries ripen until December, violets scent the woods all winter through and daffodils start blooming at Christmas or soon after. Nature here is at her most bountiful and this is indeed one of the most 'Fortunate of Isles'.

It may not be necessary to search for further treasure but truth to tell the island demands so much attention to garner her riches that there is just no time to dig for buried treasure. And there it must remain, unless, of course, we get a sign, then out will come the shovels and pickaxes again, no doubt.

The
MARINERS'
Tale

The session with the wine-glass was not the only eerie experience I had.

One of the best UFO stories I read about was in a *Reader's Digest*. It was reported that a party of some twelve WI ladies, or their American counterparts, had sighted a UFO overhead. Everyone of the twelve vouched to having seen it and all swore that they knew it to be genuine because there, painted under the body, in huge letters was the inscription 'UFO'.

I say one of the best UFO stories because the best one happened to me. The memory is so vivid that although it happened a few years ago I can recall it in every detail to this day.

Our friend Philla was staying with me, and although she was sleeping down in Jetty Cottage she will confirm that every word of what I am about to relate is true. We had spent the evening together talking, among other things, about UFOs as they were very much in the news just then and several sightings had been reported. Alone in the house but for Lucky, who was lying at the bottom of my bed, I was in a deep sleep when suddenly I was awakened by a brilliant white light flooding the room. It travelled across the window then was followed by a sudden inky blackness. I jumped out of bed and looked out of the window. Was it a vivid dream? No! there it was again — an intense bluey-white beam that swept across the house then out to the cliff edge beyond the lawn, again followed by intense blackness. Heart thumping, I peered through the window. Suddenly a broad beam of light enveloped me and the house, hovered over the lawn and border, lighting up the flowers with a deathly pallor. The target was obviously the house and the lawn.

Transfixed I waited for several minutes, trying to collect my thoughts and give some reasonable explanation for this phenonomen. I could not think of one. That it was a searchlight was apparent, but a shaft of light of that breadth could only mean that its source, if not actually on the island, must be very close by. It came neither from the seaward side nor from the land but from the eastern or left-hand side of the island, the cliffs of which were only about 100 yards from the house.

The bathroom would provide an excellent look-out as the windows were large, one facing due east, the source of the light. Holding Lucky very closely to me I crept to the bathroom. I had no sooner reached the window than the light came straight at me blinding me with its intensity. Quickly I ducked down, my face felt ashen and drained of blood, its pallor due not only to the light but, I must confess, to craven fear that I had now been seen by whoever or whatever was 'out there'. In the short periods between the probing beams I peered out into the darkness, the warmth of Lucky's body giving me comfort as well as the courage I so sorely needed. What with the constant ducking to avoid being spotted and my eyes trying to adjust from the dazzling beam that lighted up the whole bathroom to the almost tangible blackness that followed, it was some time before I saw 'IT'. 'IT' was a flashing blue lamp; not only was it flashing continuously and giving off an eerie glow but it was actually swaying to and fro and up and down *over* the sea, a few yards beyond the cliff top.

I stumbled downstairs to fetch my binoculars. Back again still clutching Lucky, I focused on this apparition. It certainly was a blue flashing lamp and now just beneath it I could make out the dark outline of something on which it was mounted. This appeared to be shaped like the old-fashioned traditional beehive, a kind of rounded turret, and it was from this, below the lamp, that the searchlight pierced the night, unmistakably focusing on the house and lawn, for having travelled slowly between these two points the light would suddenly be extinguished. The blue lamp rode aloft; it appeared to be rising and hovering over the sea. 'My God!' I cried aloud, 'it's a UFO

and it is about to take off and land on the lawn!' For the blue
lamp was now swaying from side to side and rose in the air as
though about to ascend. My heart seemed to freeze. 'We are
about to be invaded, not just by trippers from the mainland, but
by aliens from outer space,' I thought in my confused state of
mind. I clutched Lucky tighter to me. It was then in the
ensuing temporary black-out that, raking the cliff with my
binoculars, I noticed something else almost on the cliff top
itself. It was the mast of a ship. 'Good Heavens! they are landing
in force — a whole planet load of them!' I panicked; I shook so
much I could scarcely hold the binoculars. Then I pulled myself
together.

'Would spacemen come in conventional ships with masts?' I
asked myself. 'Surely they usually travel in saucers?' The
searchlight picked out the dark outline of the mast again, then
through the window which I had now opened I heard voices.
They sounded low, guttural, urgent. With a gulping sigh of
relief I realized at once that they were not beings from outer
space. Would they have human voices? Of course not. Surely
telepathy, radio beams or sign language were their means of
communication. Although not a science fiction fan I knew that
creatures from outer space are always more advanced than we
are; they would be more sophisticated than to use ordinary
human-like speech. If they were not spacemen who were they?
Who would man such a strange looking craft and search for a
suitable landing-place, for it happened that the lawn was the
only level piece of land on the whole island.

Why! The Russians of course, who else? Brainwashed by the
media and spy fiction I knew that the Russians were never up to
any good. The island was very handy for Devonport dockyard
and obviously of strategic military value to any foreign power
with evil intent. I had not read my press for nothing and I was
well up with current affairs. 'Right!' I said, 'We will fight them
on the beaches! We will fight them on the cliffs!' and with these
Churchillian phrases ringing in my ears I hurriedly dressed.
'You stay quietly here,' I admonished Lucky, shutting him in
the kitchen with a Bonio. I wasn't going to have him shot at by

the Russians — not our Lucky. Then trembling from head to foot I ventured outside. I would not disturb Philla — there was no point in two of us being frightened. I do not recall exactly what I intended to do. Certainly not a polite 'Have we met?' for I knew for certain that I had never met a Russian here. Again the historic phrase 'Something must be done,' went through my mind.

So out I went to do it, though *what* I still did not know. The blue light was still flashing as I approached the cliff top. The searchlight beamed out again showing up the ship's mast which appeared to be almost on the island itself. I neared the edge of the cliff and was armed with nothing more than a torch when out of the darkness I heard a voice shout in unmistakable Cockney accents 'Can't you get us orf yet then, mate?' to which the reply came in rich Cornish brogue: 'Tide's coming in fast. Hold on a bit and we will make it.' I almost collapsed with relief when I realized that the mast must be that of a holiday-maker's fishing boat or yacht marooned on the treacherous island rocks. The bobbing blue light belonged not to a flying saucer nor a Russian submarine, but to a lifeboat and was the equivalent of the flashing blue lamp mounted aloft police cars, a maritime innovation unknown to me.

The next day I heard that while I was trembling in my boots half Looe had a grandstand view from Hannafore of this nocturnal rescue, which was safely accomplished, shortly after my arrival on the scene.

In the morning I asked Philla if she had seen anything, for Jetty Cottage, although much nearer to all the activity, was out of direct range of the searchlight. 'Oh! yes,' said Philla, 'I saw lights flashing and wondered what all the racket was about. It kept me awake until nearly 3 o'clock.' All of which goes to show that some of us have more equable temperaments than others, and a little imagination can go a very long way; in this case as far as outer space and Russia and back in a very short time. Faster than light one could say.

This was not the only maritime incident in which the island was involved; we have had boats stranded on the dangerous rocks a number of times, especially in the summer when inexperienced holiday-makers in hired boats, drawn to the island like a magnet, venture too close and get wedged or caught on the rocks. We will then hail a passing fishing boat to get a message to the boatman in Looe harbour who, irate at losing valuable plying time, will come out to tow them back, while we meantime have taken them in our charge, for quite often they are city youngsters who find the experience quite frightening, as indeed it can be.

Although in winter there are rarely any small craft about, there have been incidents even then. One winter's morning about 6 a.m. I was having coffee by the Aga when there was a thump on the door. As it was pitch dark I wondered who on earth would be calling at that hour. 'We've been shipwrecked!' cried voices loudly as I opened the door. There stood two men. They had been out fishing and in the darkness their boat had caught on submerged rocks off the main beach. Luckily they had been able to wade ashore and make their way up to the house, where they were thankful to see a light. I entertained them to coffee until it was light, having meantime contacted Babs on the radio telephone to get someone to come and pick them up. Their boat, which was about the size of the *Islander*, some eighteen feet and broad-beamed, was stuck on the rocks for some time. Later the two fishermen came out and made temporary repairs so that it would not sink and, when the tides were high enough, they returned to tow her away. So all ended without disaster.

Not so lucky was the speedboat that tried to land here. The father of a journalist who had interviewed us was so keen to see the island for himself that he came out at the first opportunity when neither the sea nor the season was really suitable. Again it was early morning but it was light. The first I knew about the visit was again a thump on the door. Only this time a voice cried 'A man is drowning!' We both rushed down to the beach. There, in a strong-running sea, was a man clinging to the buoyancy seat which had come adrift from their sinking speedboat. We dragged our dinghy down the beach and I rowed out towards him. He was not many yards off the shore but the water was deep and rough and he was distressed, as well he might be. We got him ashore without too much difficulty and, when he had recovered from the initial shock and the swallowing of sea-water, helped him up to the house. Throwing all maidenly modesty aside I stripped off his wet clothes, rubbed him down, covered him with blankets and plied him with hot tea. I found him some jeans and a fisherman's top which luckily fitted, and both of which were Unisex, although that epithet had not then come into the language. I was able to call Babs before she left for school and Leonard came out to fetch the two men. The speedboat, when it was raised, was in a sorry state. It had skimmed over submerged rocks which had torn seven holes in its keel. Eventually it was towed to the mainland followed later by a parcel of dried clothing. So once again tragedy had been averted.

Once I was nearly shipwrecked myself.

During the time that Cecily and Doug were staying with us I spent a few days ashore with Babs in the cottage to do my Christmas shopping. Cecily, too, came over one day to go into Plymouth with us to do her Christmas shopping. The next day Leonard was to take her back to the island and bring Doug over to pick up some fuel for the boiler. I decided to take advantage of the double trip to go over to the island with Cecily, bottle home-made wine ready for the coming festivities and attend to various pottery pieces I was making. I would then go back to the mainland on Leonard's return trip from ferrying Doug and the fuel.

It was blowing a bit from the north-west, so Cecily and I donned waterproof clothing and Babs and I loaded the open boat with stores and Christmas presents and covered these up as best we could. It was quite rough when once we were out in the open sea; it was mid-December and there were no other boats to be seen, but with Leonard at the helm we had no fear. He took us into the lee of the island and all was landed safely at the jetty. There was some discussion about whether Doug should go over for the fuel as the wind was freshening, but as the direction of the wind was north-west and the weather forecast had given no change, it was decided to make the trip, so I landed and Cecily and I moved up the stores. All went well, Leonard and Doug returned with the anthracite and landed it on the beach and stored it in the boathouse meantime. As there would not be enough tide to get him back up the river for another half-hour or so, Leonard came up to the house for a cup of tea. When we returned to the beach, in that short time, with the incoming tide the wind had turned westerly and strengthened. Waves were crashing over the rocks and the boat (which, for some reason I do not recall, was not Leonard's) was full of water. Doug pumped it out but when I got into the boat it was still leaking.

Now the troubles started. Leonard managed to launch the boat, which was quite a feat, as the surf was breaking over us. She kept going broadside on and drifting towards the rocks. Leonard pushed with the boat-hook while Cecily and Doug heaved and shoved. Although it was only a ferry-boat and not as heavy as the *Islander* it took all their strength in that surging sea, and at one stage Cecily was up to her armpits in the surf. Then the rudder dropped off! After a struggle this was rescued and put back in position and we did at last get beyond the breaking rollers into the open sea. But now Leonard had another problem. As the sea was running strongly from the west the waves were catching us broadside on and steering was difficult. One felt in danger of being pitched overboard for, in an open boat of that size, the seats were only a few inches below the gunwales. There was no time to think about this danger however — there was too much to do, for the boat was now leaking badly.

'Pump as hard as you can!' called Leonard, busy navigating with great skill in the turbulent sea. I pumped like mad for our feet were slopping in water and it took all my time and strength to stop the level rising. On a calm day in summer it takes about a quarter of an hour to twenty minutes depending on the tide, from the island to the harbour; when it is rough it can take considerably longer. It certainly was going to take considerably longer today for suddenly the engine stopped. 'Can you row,'

asked Leonard, 'while I try to get the engine going?' I rather
fancied myself at being able to feather a pretty oar. There would
be no feathering today, however — I was much more likely to
catch a crab in those wild waves — or something worse, for I was
dismayed to find on picking up the oars that one of them was
only half an oar. Luckily the blade was intact and somehow or
other, by pulling on this one with the naturally weaker left arm,
I was able to keep a straight course. In between trying to get the
engine started Leonard was having to pump, for the boat began
to fill if there was any lull in the pumping.

At last he said 'It's no good! the engine is flooded.' We now
took it in turns to row and pump so that Leonard could keep
having a go at the engine. 'Are you all right?' he asked, for we
still had a long way to go. I was uncomfortably wet. I was
sitting in pools of icy water, for my waterproofs were proving no
protection from the waves that broke over us from time to time,
drenching us with spray, and the water was slopping over my
feet from the leaking boat.

It was a ludicrous situation to say the least. Here we were in
mid-December in wild seas in a small open boat that was
leaking badly, the engine stalled and just one and a half oars to
get us back to harbour and, of course, there were no other craft
about in those stormy seas to whom we could signal for help.
But with Leonard in charge I had no fear. Although then in his
sixties, he was a fine-looking man with a sailor's far-seeing blue
eyes. He had always taken a special interest in our welfare. He
was of the opinion that we were too trusting. If so it stood me
in good stead now for I had absolute faith in Leonard — all
would be well with Leonard at the helm. It was all just a big
adventure as far as I was concerned.

So when he asked if I was all right I replied, 'Well, all I can
say is that this is better than queueing for a 77 bus in London.'
Whenever I had wanted one they seemed to come in droves with
a half-hour wait in between — or so it seemed to me. As in those
far-off days I would often walk two miles rather than wait for a
bus, it was no wonder that I though the present situation

preferable — at least one had no chance of being bored. It just
did not enter my head that if the boat filled up any more — and
we had to pump really hard to stop the level from rising — the
boat might well have sunk and we with it.

At last the rocks at Hannafore, exposed by the low tide,
sheltered us from the worst of the seas running from the west.
We now made good progress and eventually reached the
harbour mouth, an hour or so after leaving the island. Leonard
got me to row the last part in the river itself on the pretext of
having another go at the engine. With hindsight I think he
wanted to show me off to the many onlookers on the quayside,
some of whom were those who had said that we would not last
out on the island more than three months.

When shopping in Plymouth I had been given a gift box by a
man demonstrating how to make them in one of the big stores.
That evening after trying to make some for Christmas I took
Toby for a walk and called on Leonard to see how he fared after
our epic journey, but he was already in bed. By the time I went
to bed I felt feverish and found that I was running a temperature
of 102. So I stayed in bed until the following evening when I got
up to make more gift boxes. I was convinced that I had caught a
germ in that Plymouth store, for living in the pure air of the
island one has no resistence against the germ-laden atmosphere
of crowded places. I probably had, but it is only as I write this
that I realize that it was much more likely that I had caught a
chill from becoming heated from the exertion of rowing and
pumping while I sat in freezing water as the icy seas sloshed over
me, especially as I have, since early childhood, always been
susceptible to sudden chills. It is only with hindsight, too, that
I realize how lucky I was to escape with only a chill, for the
following day it was discovered that the keel of the boat was
fractured and we had been in very real danger of sinking in that
winter sea.

Be that as it may, at the time I vowed that in future I would
avoid crowded stores and go shopping as little as possible — a
vow I have tried to keep from that day to this, although I must

admit that I have never been keen on shopping anyway — I much prefer the hazards of island life.

However, it says something for Leonard's maritime expertise and the confidence that he inspired, that for all these years the only danger I felt I had been in on that weekend was from the germs of overcrowded stores!

The
WINTER'S
Tale

One of the questions we are most frequently asked, apart from 'Why don't you keep sheep and cows?' is 'What is it like in the winter?' or, as a variation, 'What do you *do* with yourselves in the winter?' The simple answer to the latter is 'Quite a lot.' What we do from day to day depends on the answer to the former, for the winter for us is a season of dramatic contrasts; storm-force winds will roar across the island to be interspersed with halcyon summer-like days. Icy winds from the north will cut through one like a knife, while on the other side of the island, sheltered from the north, it may be possible to picnic in short sleeves; it is very easy to catch chills.

As our main interest is the cultivation of the land we are, like farmers, dependent on the weather and as we are entirely dependent on the state of the sea for obtaining our supplies, the services of the engineer, electrician, plumber and mason, and the delivery and collection of our all-important mail, we are obsessional about weather forecasts. We listen to the early morning shipping forecast and plan our day accordingly. The climate is exceptionally mild, similar we are told to that of the Isles of Scilly. Frost and snow are virtually unknown so the growing season is very long, and the growth of grass and weeds is continuous throughout the winter.

With the departure of summer visitors and voluntary helpers at the end of September our busy time, horticulturally, comes into its own. Harvesting which started in July, now reaches its peak, and goes well into November and even December. Now we gather the fruits of our labours: grapes, figs, sweetcorn, artichokes, apples, pears, plums, late tomatoes, marrows, courgettes, squashes, beans, main crop potatoes, late beetroot;

other root vegetables, such as chicory, carrots, swedes, parsnips and Jerusalem artichokes, will be lifted as required throughout the winter. Blackberries grow in profusion; they start to ripen in July and some crops can be picked until December if the autumn rains have not ruined them. So on every fine day we climb around the island to garner them, making fresh tracks in the now crackling bramble. High up on the hill near the chapel site the berries are particularly large and luscious, like grapes, and give rise to our fancy that the monks may have cultivated them back in the twelfth century. There are apple trees in the daffodil fields as well as in the orchard, so in a bumper year we toil until nightfall to pick them before the gales hurl the fruit to the ground.

The autumnal equinox brings gales and with them a rich harvest of seaweed, so we drag up truckloads of this to spread on the land, which we are feverishly trying to clear and dig, before the rains come. This seaweed is invaluable and has a threefold use; not only is it a fertilizer and wonderful conditioner for the soil, but a thick layer will help suppress the weeds, which would otherwise be a foot or eighteen inches high by January. It also helps to feed the voracious appetite of our six compost heaps, together with a second growth of nettles which we cut. This is all hard physical work, often in less than ideal conditions, so it is almost a therapy to clear the two greenhouses to make way for winter salads, biennials and early crops, for our sowing season begins again in January. Now is the time, too, to plant trees, shrubs and bushes; each year we extend our range of fruits and have added nectarines, kiwi fruit, worcesterberries and tayberries to our black and red currants, raspberries, gooseberries etc. When we first came we started a plantation of conifers and they have grown into magnificent trees and provide us with our Christmas tree each year. The walnut tree we planted in 1976 is now a fine specimen but has yet to produce more than embryo walnuts. We have planted other nut trees as well as peach, apricot and almond and palm trees which are Babs' especial delight. In spite of the high winds they have grown tall and luxuriantly, and are a fine sight when they come into flower. We are gradually extending the vineyard too, and now that we have established an asparagus bed, the feathery foliage must be cut down and more seaweed brought up to spread here, for asparagus thrives on this treatment.

Beans are salted down, chicory and endive blanched, apples and potatoes graded and stored. The aroma of spices and the pungent smell of vinegar pervades the kitchen as produce is made into chutneys, pickles and relishes. Elderberries, blackberries and the fruit we have grown will now be made into jams, jellies, sweet pickles and wines. As November merges into December the heady scent of apples mingles with the warm smell of freshly baked bread. Wine ferments merrily in the kitchen as cheese- and yoghurt-making is in progress. The bees have been fed for the winter and now we label and store away the delectable jars of honey.

Somehow or other we must find time to deal with accounts and tax returns and answer the letters we receive with pleasure worldwide, for seemingly everyone loves an island. Time must be made, too, for printing our stationery and maps, and designing and printing our Christmas cards; cut stencils, duplicate leaflets and deal with correspondence connected with next year's conservation volunteers and would-be cottagers. We try to snatch time for our cherished crafts, for I have pots, chessmen and shire-horses to be decorated, glazed and fired in the pottery, and marquetry chess boards to be made. Babs has semi-precious stones from the sea-shore and innumerable shells awaiting her deft fingers. Wood is waiting to be carved and there are many more crafts that our itching, but too busy fingers are hoping, but often in vain, to make.

As autumn gales are succeeded by winter storms, we forage for driftwood. Sometimes we alight with great triumph on timber that is fit for carpentry for making into benches, tables and shelving, or choice pieces that lend themselves to carving. Often tree trunks are thrown up by the sea and these can be chopped or sawn into logs for our fire. Storm-force winds scream through the woods, uprooting thirty- and forty-foot trees, toppling them like ninepins. Every possible day in the depth of winter we are up in the woods, dragging, sawing and chopping tree trunks and branches and hauling down truck-loads of logs. Several times we have had to hack and chop our way through fallen trees that have blocked our path before we could reach the beach to meet Tony Pengelly in the *Islander* when he brings supplies and our precious mail, and to reach the generator, which has to be tended daily. The winds are sometimes so strong that we have to stumble along the path in a crouching position for fear of being lifted bodily and hurled over the cliff. It can be dangerous, too, to lean against the wind for a gust that stops suddenly can send one sprawling headlong. It is in the winter that the freshwater pump down in the cliff face develops airlocks and other troubles, and slippery rocks and piles of seaweed several feet deep have to be traversed to tend it, often in biting winds and lashing rain.

The island now is as remote from Looe as though it were in mid-Atlantic; a jewel certainly, but set in turbulent seas. Giant rollers race past, spume flying in their wake, to break on the shore and rocks in towering cascades of spray. The screams of the gulls mingle with the howling of the wind and the thunder of the sea, and huge scuds of foam fly over the house and are driven from one end of the island to the other.

It was in such a day as this in 1974 that it was given out on the radio that owing to the conjunction of sun, moon and earth, the highest tides for 300 years were to be expected. This meant, on the mainland, the danger of widespread flooding and, on the island, the fear of losing the two boats we kept high up on the beach. These were tied up alongside the boathouse, tight up against the wooded cliff adjoining the path. We reckoned that the boathouse had been there close on a hundred years for we had been given pictures taken at the turn of the century showing it there then. It must, in that time, have withstood many onslaughts; it was large, some thirty feet by twelve feet, solidly built and housing several outboard motors, diesel drums, oars, rollocks and other impedimenta to do with boats. It should be safe enough.

The boats were another matter as they could be sucked out by the sea if it came up that high. One was a heavy clinker boat, with an inboard motor, which we had bought under Leonard's guidance so that Babs and I could ferry ourselves, and it replaced a metal boat that had been lost off our mooring in a gale; the other was an eight-foot, glass-fibre dinghy, a very light craft, used mainly as a tender for the *Islander*, which was moored in the river in Looe harbour. It was imperative that they were made as fast as possible. Knot-tying was not my forte — something about its intricacy eludes me — but I had had one unexpected success with a great-granny knot that I had once invented in an emergency, so I diligently tied the two boats to the trees at the foot of the cliffs, great-granny style, and hoped that they had a reasonable chance of withstanding the strain and pull of the sea if it encroached that far.

On the beach was an enormous barge. It was more like a flat-bottomed boat with four sides supported by substantial posts at each corner. It had been used in the past for towing heavy machinery and furniture and was very solid indeed, measuring some 25 feet long, 12 feet wide and 4 feet deep. It was half buried in the sand from the onslaught over the years of countless storms and, as it was absolutely immovable, had proved invaluable to us as a beach anchorage for securing our boats. Now, however, the boats stood a better chance from the encroaching sea high up under the cliff.

The morning of the highest tide I looked out of the bedroom window facing seaward and my mouth fell open, for mountainous seas towering higher than the cliffs were crashing on the cliff top itself, then sweeping from one side of the promontory to the other. The flagstaff was no longer there. The tumultuous seas had uprooted the tabernacle supporting the flagstaff, and hurled it from the southern side of the promontory over to the cliff top on the eastern side. This was just a hundred yards or so from the house. Spray was driven across the lawn like a blizzard and great scuds of foam as large as one's fist clung to the branches of trees. What would it be like on the beach facing the mainland where the boats were? I raced down the path to the beach but to my relief all was still intact. The sea was swirling round the bows of the two boats and was actually lapping the side of the boathouse, but the moment of danger was past. Or was it? Sometimes after the highest spring tide, we have often, unpredictably, experienced an even higher one. This may be due to atmospheric pressure, for this can increase the height of the tide. Whatever the reason it can happen, so I tied some more knots in the ropes and dragged the boats tight up against the cliff. When I checked at high tide that night all was still secure.

The next morning, however, the sea was a scene of violent tumult: mountainous seas were still crashing over the cliff top at the back of the house and great breakers were thundering past Jetty Bay, the spume streaming behind in their wake for hundreds of yards. As I hurried down to the beach an incredible sight met my horrified gaze. Diesel drums were being tossed thirty feet in the air like ping-pong balls at a fair; a long line of debris swept at breakneck speed towards Rame Head — the contents of the boathouse — and before me was a scene of utter desolation, for of the boathouse, boats and barge there was no sign. Part of the path, too, had disappeared and left a six-foot drop to the beach below where the surf still sucked greedily. The raging seas beat against the cliff where once the boathouse had been. It and its contents were lost for ever, and nothing was seen again of the boats and the barge, although over the years the sea did give back the odd anchor, pulley, chain or other metal objects.

The only small consolation I had on that disastrous day was that I could have done no more to save the boats, for the frayed ropes still hung from the trees with the knots intact — it was the ropes themselves which had been torn apart by the force of the sea.

Every coast in the country suffered from those calamitous seas. Babs told me that the flooding in West Looe made the bridge impassable so that she could not get to school. At West Looe the swollen river overflowed its banks and cars were swept from the quayside over the road to the shops, and boats were dragged from their mooring on to the car park. She had heard that a man had swum in the streets in East Looe, another had rowed down the street in Fowey, and that fish had been caught in Boots, the chemists, there.

The winter takes its toll in other ways. Tiles fly off the roof every year — once thirteen went in one go leaving a gaping hole in the gable roof. Luckily this was over the hall and a row of buckets dealt with the continual stream of rain until Jack could get over to replace the tiles. On one never-to-be-forgotten occasion the bathroom flat roof took off and the rain seeped through and poured down in so many places that it was not possible to reach the wash-basin without an umbrella — except that we possessed no umbrella, for it is not standard equipment on windswept islands. We solved *that* problem by drilling a hole in the ceiling so that the rain would find its outlet in one steady stream and thus could be trapped in a dustbin. This we emptied at intervals until the gale subsided and Jack could get over to make a temporary repair, for this was a major replacement job, requiring, as it transpired, the services of a roofing expert experienced in the use of boiling pitch! Jack Tambling would come out in any possible weather, often braving stormy seas to replace tiles and make other emergency repairs. How we came to know him in the first place is a tale in itself.

Landslides are a common hazard around the coastline of Britain as the sea gradually erodes the coast. The island is no exception and there have been several falls since we have been here, making dangerous undercuts and leaving some of the cliff paths perilously close to the edge. One day after a series of severe south-west gales I heard a dull roar followed by an ominous thump. On investigation I found to my horror that there had been a landslide above the jetty beach, some twenty-five yards from the house and a bare two yards from the edge of the main path. Tons of earth and cliff had fallen and completely obliterated the pump-house in the cliff below.

This was a disaster indeed, for our only supply of fresh water was now inaccessible. When I told Babs on the radio telephone she went post-haste to the Council. Yes! they would do what they could to help, but it would be costly for us, as the rates did not cover this sort of contingency. When the weather calmed somewhat, out came a team of council workmen headed by their foreman, Jack Tambling. A shy, diffident Cornishman, he now showed his enormous courage. He hammered an iron stake into the daffodil field directly above the cliff fall, tied a rope to this, belayed himself, then casually stepped over the cliff edge as though he were stepping outside his front door, and climbed down the perpendicular precipice to the cliff fall some thirty feet below. The team now toiled away shifting the tons of earth and rock under Jack's direction and with his help. It seemed an impossible task, but after several days of navvying eventually the pump-house was excavated and the petrol pump lifted up out of the well where it had fallen, spilling oil and petrol into our precious spring water. The tunnel into the cliff now had to be cleared and the pump-house and the steps leading up to it completely rebuilt.

Unfortunately none of this was covered by insurance as a landslide was deemed an 'Act of God'. However, a tree trunk had fallen into the well from the cliff top, too, and for some technical reason God was not held responsible for this, and the assessor, over a glass or so of home-made wine — for I had no fresh water to offer tea or coffee — allowed us 25 per cent of the cost instead of nothing.

We had always had trouble with the petrol pump, and even when it functioned perfectly, it was no fun in the depth of winter to slither over piles of seaweed and rocks and clamber up the steps into the cliff face to start the engine. This entailed pulling a cord, similar to starting a motor-mower. If the engine was in a sullen mood and the tugs consequently became sharper, one was in danger of falling head-over-heels backwards down the steep steps on to the rocks below. Added to this was the ever present hazard of being drenched with icy water when the pipes jerked apart or split with the sudden force of water. We decided, therefore, that we would put the insurance money towards an electric pump. As this could be started from a switch in the house this would solve all our problems — or would it? Well not quite, as we were to discover. Air-locks and other non-events still necessitate winter visits to the pump-house, and, of course, all our eggs were now in one basket, for if the generator grinds to a halt, the pump is unusable. Not all can be perfect in an imperfect world, so we do our best to keep the water-storage tanks in the woods full to the brim, but this is not possible during a drought, which can often last from spring until autumn, the effects being felt until after Christmas. Paradise does have its problems!

When Jack left working for the Council he became self-employed and, as well as carrying out our emergency jobs, he became for a period the official postman, ferried the diesel oil and other supplies and transported Babs for her rare weekends and holidays on the island. During the Christmas holidays the big problem was when she should return to the mainland, and it seemed that we spent most of the second week of her holiday with our ears glued to the radio listening to the shipping and weather forecasts in case her visit had to be suddenly curtailed.

One particular Christmas the weather turned foul almost as soon as Babs had landed. The gales continued the whole holiday period, at times reaching storm force. Luckily they abated towards the end of the holiday, but the aftermath left a great surge of wild seas breaking on the beaches. Jack had spoken on the radio telephone and it was arranged that he would come out and size up the situation to see if a landing were possible. It was a bright sunny day, so we felt optimistic as the white-crested rollers, crowned by the blue sky overhead, sparkled in the sunshine. Paradoxically it seems really menacing when those same seas rush at you from under leaden skies, the wind stinging your face with icy rain.

As we approached the surf we espied the *Islander*, a lone craft, gleaming white in the sunlight. It was bucking in the great troughs and at the helm stood the indomitable oilskin-clad figure of Jack. Babs, desperate to make it to the boat, now that Jack had braved the rough seas, reckoned that if she could wade out beyond the surf she could board the *Islander* there; it would prevent the danger of it going broadside on in the surf and getting smashed up on the rocks. Why we considered that she could withstand the raging breakers I do not recall, but ever prudent, we had thoughtfully brought a rope with us. Babs tied this round her waist and I belayed it round mine, in the best mountaineering manner. 'I am coming out beyond the surf on a rope,' yelled Babs above the sound of the crashing waves, as she ploughed into the sea, 'and you can pick me up from there.' Beneath his sou'wester we could see the look of horror on Jack's face. 'Don't you dare! You will be *drowned*!' he bellowed, and with that he turned the boat about and made for the harbour, the only way he knew to stop Babs from plunging further into the broiling sea. A receding breaker sucked round Babs' knees nearly toppling her over and dragging her back with it. I gave a tremendous tug and leaned back on the rope as though I was trying to land a fish and Babs staggered ashore to spend an extra day on the island.

The next day Jack was able to pick her up and take her ashore without incident as the sea, if not exactly calm, was manageable. Hazardous and unpredictable as the sea is, it was the only time Babs was adrift on the island in all the twelve years she was teaching in Looe, mainly because she usually curtailed her holidays as a precaution in case, as in this instance, the weather forecast was not a reliable enough guide. Paradoxically if she had lived up on Bodmin Moor on the mainland she would have been 'adrift' quite a number of times during those years, for staff who lived there were cut off by snowdrifts on a number of occasions during the winter months and were unable to make it to school.

Those Christmas holidays were very precious to us for it was, and still is, the only time we take a 'holiday'. We have the usual chores to do, the generator and water pump must be attended to, and Christmas cooking makes for busyness as for others, but we do relax mentally. We have this fantasy that from Christmas Eve until Twelfth Night we are cruising in a yacht to exotic places, and plot our 'course' according to the weather. We play Scrabble, read, listen to music, watch TV and enjoy the company of our pets. We cannot entertain our friends or relations; we are too remote and the danger of their being cut off is too great. Local friends have taken short trips out to see us but the possibilities are rare. The weather varies so much that we never know if we shall have to batten down the hatches, so to speak, or if the weather may be spring-like. Christmas 1983, for instance, we were able to have a barbecue and two picnics; we actually celebrated New Year's Day with a picnic high up on the hill in warm sunshine. When you live on the job it is difficult to take time off, and Christmastide with its special atmosphere is the only time when we can do this without the nagging thoughts of jobs to be done.

Christmas over, it is back to the land, and no more fine feasts at the Captain's table. Traditionally one can plant early potatoes on the island on Boxing Day. Afraid of compacting the soil we usually leave this for a few weeks, for the worst of the winter weather is still to come. Although it is only a matter of weeks before our spring, the storms can be so severe that the time seems incredibly long, possibly because we experience the winter in depth rather than in actual length. Now is the time for sowing and greenhouse work. Christmas or not, tree-clearing and log-sawing go on daily, if the storms are not wreaking havoc in the woods, for on those days it would be dangerous to venture there for fear of falling trees. Loads of seaweed are now brought up for potato planting as well as for the compost heaps. As soon as the soil is fit I dig hundreds of feet of trenches ready for the potatoes and later the runner beans. Babs and I then line them with comfrey, compost and seaweed. As soon as possible we start planting the early potatoes and rotavate the land that has gone back to nature over the winter. Daffodils start blooming in January, so soon we are feverishly alternating between daffodils, greenhouse and the land. If we do not cut the five lawns and many grass verges it must be done soon or a scythe will be necessary. In any case all the grass has to be raked up and added to the compost heaps.

In between Babs deals with a welter of correspondence about the working holidays; it is like a jigsaw puzzle as she tries to fit applicants in, knowing that some will cancel, and others alter dates; then the jigsaw will have to be started all over again. I print our headed paper and cut stencils for information sheets and the like, which we will both run off on our ancient and unreliable duplicator. Longingly we think of our neglected crafts, but now and again we take time to throw a pot, do some woodwork, shellcraft or whatever, if only as a refreshment for the spirit.

All too soon it will be spring and we are not quite ready, as we never are, as each season nudges into the next. The first visitors will soon appear and we must gear our thoughts and energies to our preparation for them. So the cycle goes on.

More than one visitor has said to us at the end of the summer season, 'I expect you will be glad when we all go and you can put your feet up,' little realizing that they are merely a pattern superimposed on the fabric of our island life, albeit with the passage of time they have become interwoven. Some with more perception have said, 'How do you put up with us, intruding on your lives?' Others ask 'What do you do for holidays?' and when we say we have none some will say, 'But you don't need holidays living in a beautiful place like this!' They would do *anything*, they say, to exchange their lives for ours. But would they? We understand their envy but doubt if they understand the responsibilities and hardships involved. When you live on the job it really is essential to get away for a break if only to recoup your vitality and recharge your mental and physical batteries. Not all understand this and think that if you live in a beautiful place, in some magical way you never get tired, never get worried, nor overwhelmed with day-to-day problems; that somehow it cannot be so bad. Why not? I have yet to hear of anyone who finds that a tooth aches any the less by a blue lagoon in the South Seas than in a crowded city — except of course that if you live in the latter a dentist is more accessible. An electricity cut, whether due to 'industrial action' or the breakdown of your own generator, plunges you into darkness as black on an island as in a city, except that if it is your own generator you have to go down at dead of night, perhaps in a howling gale and slashing rain, to try to do something about it — and there are no shops to fly to for candles or paraffin.

Many visitors who sit on top of the island in the hot summer sunshine, fanned by refreshing sea breezes or who stroll along the cliff paths admiring the magnificent views and the myriad colours of the translucent sea, do not realize when they envy us that no one will ever meet us there during the months of summer; that the only time we can enjoy a carefree jaunt or a casual stroll is during our hard-won Christmas holiday on our mythical cruise to faraway places. It is then that we also can appreciate the sheer joy of our island paradise. We feel, on those rare summer days in the depth of winter that sparkle like a jewel in the darkness, that we are on another planet; that we are privileged for a short spell to be part of the timeless universe, where there is no beginning, no end, only a magical limitless 'now'.

The
AUTHOR'S
Tale

'What made you want to write?' 'Had you written much before your book was published?' 'How do you find time to write *anything*?' The first two of these oft repeated questions I will attempt to answer here; the short answer to the third is by starting the day at 5 a.m.

Writing is a solitary occupation, but in my case it is not so. Lucky helps me. After we lost our splendid border collie, Kim, Babs heard that Lucky needed a home as his owner, a Marine Commando, was being posted to Malta. We were delighted, therefore, to welcome someone who was almost an exact replica of Toby, even to his tightly curled and jaunty tail. Partly a smooth-haired terrier, partly labrador, he is golden brown with an immaculate white front, paws and tail-tip. He has the same gentlemanly manners as Toby, too, allowing ladies through doors first, and letting his adorable but greedy young friend Emma, a black collie/labrador cross, share his meals and have the best place by the fireside. He does not sing as Toby did, but he speaks and most eloquently too. He has a repertoire of notes and tones that express a comprehensive range of emotions and comments — he has been known to make a downright condemnation if a politician on TV appears to act churlishly. A born actor, he will freely give encores if any clever action of his is applauded. He thinks things out for himself too. Obviously trained by the Marine Commando to attend to the calls of nature in the garden border, although only nine months old when he came here, he soon made other arrangements. He marches the quarter of a mile or so down the path to the beach, heads for the far eastern corner of the shore and uses the point where waves from the east and west meet and will thus obliterate all traces of doggy visits. He then marches home again. Visitors have noticed these expeditions and are amazed to learn that this contribution to a pollution-free island is entirely his own idea.

It is his own idea, too, to sit with me here while I write — here in Jetty Cottage. Sue, the silver-grey cat, who took over from Joan, has decided that she is going to help me write the book, too, and Emma sometimes wants to be in on the act. My table is beautifully crafted from driftwood by Andrew Giles and Adam Kelly, two of our most stalwart and regular helpers, who spent many hours fining and polishing it to perfection. By contrast the chair on which I sit is an elegant antique. As well as the impedimenta of writing I have a camera nearby, for early on a summer's morning the view across the bay, through the window opposite, is one of ever-changing beauty; the rising sun pierces the morning mist and the limpid sea, stirred by a slight breeze, ripples in the sunlight. With luck a fishing-boat will sail across the sparkling pathway of the sun and, framed by a dark hanging bough of a tree on the cliff top a few yards from the window, it is like a Japanese painting and I will capture the moment on film. If only I were an artist!

But I must write. Lucky sitting beside me will see to that. He joined us when *We Bought An Island* was published and he appeared in the first TV programme made to launch the book here on the island. This was only a matter of days after he took up residence. He was determined, therefore, that this, the sequel, should be written and he nudges me down here if I should falter. But he has other duties to perform too; there is the whole island to be policed — he and Emma know instantly if anyone lands. He must keep a watchful eye on Emma, too, help Babs and encourage the helpers then, handsome and charming, he will accompany Babs and Emma to greet the visitors. Tilly, our magnificent long-haired light tortoise-shell cat, runs her own escort service, meeting and seeing guests off the boat and accompanying them on walks up the hill and over the rocks. Samantha, the dark tortoise-shell one, truly splendid with emerald jewels for eyes, is too languid to take an interest in people, or the book, and is often referred to as Samantha, Lady

Bertram. Later Lucky will return to keep me informed of any events that require my presence.

It is said that everyone has a book in them, and countless people will tell you that they could write a book about their experiences — if only they had the time. When I first decided to be a writer I did not have a book in me, nor had I much in the way of experiences, although there was an enormous amount of time ahead to write about them, for I was just six years old. There was no doubt about my future career. When asked at school what we wanted to be when we grew up, among the would-be nurses, ballerinas, actresses and circus riders, I declared grandiously: 'I am going to be an author.' No 'want' about it — just a declaration of intent. It may seem odd, therefore, that I had retired more years than I care to acknowledge before I actually became one. Why this lengthy interval? To explain it is necessary to go back a bit — almost a lifetime, in fact.

Although I never gave up the idea of being a writer, other pursuits claimed my attention too. Reading was obsessional. Photography had caught me in its magic spell since the age of four, inspiring me to make my own camera around the age of ten. With a cricket-loving father and brothers, games became a creed. Classes in gymnastics, dancing and eurhythmics were part of the fabric of early childhood and music became an enduring passion. One could escape at the piano into a solitary enchanted world. Mother encouraged me in all these pursuits, especially music — the music teacher did too, and when she said I was her best pupil, I considered the idea that perhaps, as well as becoming an author, I would be a concert pianist, too. The world was certainly my oyster. It was early days yet, however, for I had not yet reached double figures in age.

As a first step towards authorship, my friend Ethel and I produced a magazine, written entirely by ourselves, apart from one story which we accepted from her brother. This magazine did not go down at all well with the Principal of our private school where we were flogging it at one penny a copy. Endeavouring as she was, with indifferent success, to instil in her charges ladylike qualities and accomplishments, she disapproved of Bessie Bunter, who was the heroine of most of our stories. She, according to her, was no lady. The magazine was banned.

Showing the determination that is essential if one is to become a genius, Ethel and I now turned our creative urge to play-writing. We wrote, produced and acted the main parts in all our plays, auditioning among our favoured friends for the lesser roles. These were open-air productions performed in our garden. This was not popular with those who had been turned down for bit parts, especially when we draped the end of the garden with sheets, to prevent gatecrashers or prying eyes from enjoying free entertainment. Babs, who now appeared on the scene for the first time, but was still a toddler, was considered too young to pay and was allowed in free. Nepotism is not only practised in high places! Our stunning performances were then given to the accompaniment of jeers, boos and cat-calls from the young ladies and gentlemen who had taken up their stance on the other side of the barricade, and who far outnumbered the paying members of the audience. In spite of their mixed reception these open-air plays were a regular feature until, at the age of thirteen, Ethel left the district and I moved to another school.

Here my literary efforts, which had graduated from episodes in the life of Bessie Bunter, became more officially acceptable. Prizes were won, and the editorship of the school magazine conducted with much pride. As far as homework was concerned I wrote unceasingly on subjects such as history, geography and literature, happily giving up much of my leisure and holidays to them, but neglecting other subjects. It seemed a waste of time to compose in Latin and French when there was so much to be said in English. Consequently my scholastic achievements were somewhat lopsided and school reports appeared to be written about two different pupils. Nevertheless our austere Headmistress, eagle-like with her aristocratic nose and flowing black gown, inspiring awe and admiration in both pupils and parents, ordained that I was destined for Oxford and an academic career. At that time a university education was not the general passport to careers as it is today, and was not generally pursued by girls unless, as I thought, they were bluestockings. I viewed with horror the prospect of a narrow academic life. In any case I had already made up my mind that I was going to be a journalist. This decision had a frozen reception. Anything less than a Bursarship, Exhibition, or Scholarship, with an Hons. Degree at Oxbridge and a fine string of letters after one's name, to be embellished in gold on the Scroll of Honour in the School Entrance Hall, was considered, one felt, fit only for the compost heap.

I was more than agreeably surprised therefore, when the school advanced me the fee to take a correspondence course in journalism when I left. It was a well-known School of Journalism with a good reputation, but I did not care for the lessons at all. At that time I fancied myself as an amalgam of Robert Louis Stevenson, Thomas Hardy, J.M. Barrie, with a dash of the Charles Lamb, and Hazlitt, plus, in my finer moments, a touch of the Beaumont and Fletcher; I was also inclined sometimes, like Walter de la Mare's Traveller knocking on moonlit doors, to ask if 'anyone was there?' and giving my own fanciful answers. The course did not cater for these literary aspirations. The lessons were full of useful tips on salesmanship, how to aim at particular markets, and a realistic attitude, that with all the ignorance and arrogance of youth I despised. So I sent the money back.

I would get a job in a newspaper office. But it was the time of the depression, and there were no jobs of any kind. I bombarded editorial offices, but to no avail. Desperate for a job I even applied for that of telephonist, but was turned down on account of the fact that I could not pronounce the letter 'R', a defect that had given me a poor showing in French, and was probably due to the time when I travelled by pram and my brothers, fighting over who should have the honour of pushing me, let the pram roll away — a split tongue being the consequence.

Then unexpectedly came a reply from the Editor of *Pearson's Weekly*. They had no job, but would be pleased to interview me to give advice. There were two other people as well as the Editor at the interview. They said that the best thing was for me to write free-lance along the lines they specified and then to submit the articles to them. They outlined their market requirements, and the kind of material they wanted, and kindly gave me a great deal of advice and encouragement.

Thrilled beyond belief I spent all my time scribbling away. Meantime I still needed a job. Here again the school helped. The Headmistress arranged an interview for me with the Headmistresses' Association for a post with the newly formed and prestigious ICI and I became an invoice clerk at 25s. per week. We were very busy and, over a long period worked overtime. In those days there was no payment for overtime, but we were allowed to claim for a meal. Usually we had Welsh rarebit costing 1s. for we did not want to overcharge the firm, but sometimes, greatly daring, we had buck rarebit — i.e., with an egg on it, and this, with a cup of tea cost 1s. 6d. I used to get very tired and after a time my music began to suffer and memorizing became more difficult. I continued to write, however, on the lines suggested by the Editor of *Pearson's Weekly*. Somewhere I had read that it was a mistake to send off anything one had written, red-hot; it should be put aside for an interval, then brought out for later appraisal. I wanted to produce my very best for the revered Editor of *Pearson's Weekly*, so I decided that my masterpieces should be put on ice for six months.

Six months later I had the shock of my life. The sage, whoever it was, who had suggested this idea, had given the most salutary advice that could help a young aspiring writer. I was appalled at what I had written. It was immature, schoolgirlish, self-concious, pompous even. No one at *Pearson's* would want to read or publish that rubbish. I tore the whole lot up. Whether it was wise to be my own mentor I shall never know, but I do remember deciding that the world must await the flowering of my genius for a few more years yet. I needed, I decided, experience of Life with a capital 'L' before I put pen to paper again, for publication that is.

So at the age of nineteen I made the momentous decision that I would not write again until the age of thirty. Why thirty, one wonders? When I was very young my ambition was to reach the age of eleven, mainly because a pair of twins in a favourite magazine had the most fantastic adventures at that age. Having reached the age of eleven the next leap forwards was the desire to be thirty. This because a glamourous lady detective of that age spent her time, in the pages of a film magazine, solving the most amazing crimes. From then on thirty years old had an alluring image. By that age, I now thought, I would have shed my gawkish schoolgirl outlook and emerged a *soignée femme fatale*, endowed, of course, with penetrating powers of detection and the ability to write with a pen dipped in liquid gold.

One might conjecture from all this fantasizing that I should find my niche as a lady writer of detective stories. Not so. Life with a capital 'L' did in fact take over, culminating, before I reached that magical age, with the outbreak of the Second World War. Well, the sort of life that appealed to me anyway. Some time after the age of twenty I regretfully gave up thoughts of becoming a concert pianist; partly because, with continuing overtime, I could not memorize whole sonatas and partly because even I, with my grandiose ideas, realized it was not something one could become in one's spare time, especially when that was in short supply.

Photography was a different matter; although exacting, it was flexible in its demands on one's time. I joined a Camera Club, later attended photographic classes at Morley College with my brother Trevor, and for good measure classes at Regent Street Polytechnic where my enthusiasm landed me with the job of Secretary of the Group. All these involved photographic expeditions and I worked far into the night in my dark-room at home. I had work exhibited, won some prizes and awards and hoped that eventually I might become a photo-journalist.

The drawback to becoming anything at all was the diversity of interests that took my fancy. Mountaineering lured me to the Alps and I have to this day my ice-axe notched with the number of peaks climbed that were over 10,000 feet. Brief weekend visits were made to the Lake District to climb there and take photographs. Weekends that were not devoted to hiking round different parts of the country with the Mountaineering Club were spent on other outdoor activities: Youth Hostelling, playing hockey, tennis, cricket and cycling. I went on lone cycling jaunts; once for a whole week. There was a purpose, apart from exploring the countryside and taking photographs; I was compiling a dossier of literary associations in Surrey. Fanny Burney's residence in the county, William Cobbett's *Rural Rides*, George Meredith's and Keats' association with Box Hill — Jane Austen's famous picnic there in *Emma*. These and many more were investigated, visited and written up in a large alphabetically indexed book I was keeping.

Box Hill had other attractions, too. My schoolgirl friend Tommy and I knew a group of young men who were involved in a Red Indian cult. This meant sleeping out on Box Hill and living a pure and wholesome life. We were made honorary members and I was given the appellation 'Minnehaha' and we partook of Indian-type food under the stars.

Working in London had many advantages and we were able to attend performances of *Hiawatha* at the Albert Hall, as well as the *Proms* and many other concerts, for which we queued happily. Theatre going in the 'gods' was a regular pursuit, and Babs, who had now caught up a bit age-wise, and I were devotees of Sadler's Wells and the Old Vic.

There was no subject that could not be studied at evening classes. Musical Appreciation conducted by a Professor of Music was particularly enjoyed, for as I now acknowledged that I should not be gracing the concert platforms of the world, I wished to applaud with informed intelligence those who did. Spanish was tried to roll out the elusive 'R's but was soon given up as a disaster; bookkeeping, to help my career, was found to be incredibly boring when there were so many more exciting things to do. I joined a Language Circle to refurbish my neglected French, but as all the other members were foreigners trying to learn English this proved to be stalemate, and I retired to be taught German by a linguist friend. This proved a much easier language to learn, as unlike the excitable Latins, the Germans seemed to pronounce each word and did not run streams of words into each other in a cacophony of unintelligible gibberish. Perhaps unexpectedly, cookery classes were attended with great enthusiasm. There seemed to be something creative and magical in transforming an assortment of ordinary, everyday ingredients into something, delectable both to eye and palate, that could give pleasure to others. Furthermore it had been no part of the curriculum at my schools — apparently future ladies or academics were not expected to eat unless someone else prepared and set the food before them. Elocution classes were joined partly because prizes had been gained for this in the past but also with the idea of dealing with the troublesome 'R's and to help with Amateur Dramatics. I belonged to the ICI Players, the Sutton and Cheam Amateur Dramatic Society and later attended Evening Drama Classes run by Babs, who had a great flair for acting and was an Adjudicator for Drama Festivals.

Sacrosanct, however, were the classes held at the City Literary Institute on The Craft of Writing. I attended courses over several years, did the exercises set and meticulously filled many notebooks. These I still have and they are valid today. It was possible to fit in yet another Photographic class on the same evening and in the coffee interval I met a lady who earned her living sticking labels on wine bottles. She gave me the benefit of her expertise which later came in very useful when I took up wine-making.

With promotion came the move to IC House, where there was a fine gymnasium and indoor sports facilities. Here I took up badminton (and later squash), rifle shooting and fencing. Foreign travel became important. Europe was explored by buying a ticket at Victoria, then once across the Channel, sleeping on the luggage rack of the third-class compartment, as the seats were so hard, until we reached Italy, Bavaria or wherever. When cruises became available for other than the wealthy and quite cheap cruising holidays were possible, I persuaded Tommy to try one with me. Our senior secretary lent me the money to buy several evening outfits which she said I would need, and off we set on our big adventure in the *Doric*, bound for Lisbon, Gibraltar and Algiers. It was a bitter disappointment. Too many people everywhere and too little time to explore faraway places, it seemed to me. We danced the night away, but I could do that at home, and the trips ashore, which were the *raison d'être* as far as I was concerned, were all too short and one was surrounded by other tourists. There was only one adventure. A doctor and his patient became our escorts for the cruise. They went to a belly dance in Algiers but would not take us as they considered it unsuitable. Furious, we decided we would explore Algiers ourselves that evening. It soon became obvious that this was not approved of by the local male population who tried to chase us away with loud cries of indignation. Soon we were pursued by hundreds of white-robed Arabs and, breathless, we only just made it back to the ship.

The following year I took to the mountains having been lured there by the *National Geographical Magazine* which had on one of its front covers a picture of a mountain in Austria crowned by a fairytale castle; but Tommy, who had become an addict, goes cruising still whenever she can.

Life was becoming crowded. Lunch-times were allocated very carefully. Mondays were spent in the Westminister Library; Tuesdays at chamber music concerts given in Christ Church; Wednesdays, browsing in a bookshop or a work-out in the gym, according to the weather; Thursdays were given up to exploring any part of London within reach. The idea was to walk in a different direction each time going as far afield as possible. The places ranged from as far apart as Blackfriars and the Tate Gallery. This last became a favourite port of call, as there was just time to study one picture in detail on each visit. Friday I graciously joined my friends for lunch. They lunched together every day and were inclined to think that I was anti-social. Nevertheless the bonds remained firm and one came to the island recently to see me.

Evenings were even more crowded. Immediately after leaving the office I would play badminton, or take part in some other activity in the bowels of IC House, have a shower, go on to an evening class or concert and finish up at a dance or party — arriving home around 1 a.m. where a rather sad-looking dinner awaited me in the oven. To fit in the obsessive reading I would on occasion, with my season ticket, board a train on a newly formed loop line and travel round and round to London and back until my book was finished, that way avoiding distractions of any kind.

Perhaps the biggest problem was fitting in various boy friends without becoming too committed. One had given me his course on Pelmanism, but that did not provide a solution; another gave me a pack of fortune telling cards, which, though they gave me the reputation for being clairvoyant, did not predict the outcome or advise me. The fact was that although romance was essential to me, my idea of it was based on Sir Thomas Malory's *Le Morte d'Arthur* and Spenser's *The Faerie Queen*. Diet of this sort of literary fare had inculcated in me, early on, high-flown ideas that were not compatible with those of young men, however personable and indeed chivalrous, whose aim was the altar, children and the quiet domestic scene, or prospective mothers-in-law who would ply me with articles 'for your bottom drawer'. I viewed with alarm the domestic constrictions of marriage and was of the opinion that some people were more suitable for the wedded state than others — and I did not feel so suited. I wished, too, for a more exciting life, and yearned to explore faraway places. Once when I read in the newspaper about a forthcoming expedition to the Antarctic I wrote offering my services as a cook/photographer. The courteous reply said that unfortunately the expedition was not recruiting ladies. It was just as well for I never could stand the cold.

When I reached the magical age of thirty I found that the complexity of reconciling these problems with multifarious pursuits and earning a living left little time for the sedentary occupation of writing, but in addition, I had a war on my hands.

Although this is by no means intended as a potted autobiography of those stirring times, for that would take a tome or two, there are some aspects that do have a bearing on the long dormant period of authorship that, like a volcano, erupted from time to time.

As I was fortunate enough to have a straight eye and a steady hand, rifle shooting had produced gold medals, silver cups, an assortment of awards, the honour of shooting for Surrey at Bisley and the accolade of 'Master Shot'. On the outbreak of war my ladies' team and I were in fact engaged in a postal match with the Polish ladies' team. That we had not received their return set of target-cards struck us with a chill of foreboding as we hastily packed our gear to move from our London Office to offices in huts on the factory site of ICI Plastics Factory at Welwyn, Herts. Here we were tracked down by a photographer sent by the *Daily Mirror*, for we had recently won a National Competition. As a result of this publicity a 'friendly' match — could it have been otherwise with those lethal weapons in our hands? — was arranged with a regiment stationed nearby and awaiting embarkation for France. I do not recall who did the challenging, but I do remember the Colonel showing me how to use a .303 rifle as I had never used one of this calibre before. I did not care for it very much for the recoil thumped one's shoulder painfully. However, much to my consternation, we won.

I was convinced by this that we should now lose the war. In any case I thought, our superior marksmanship was being wasted in the country's hour of need. So now at long last I put pen to paper, hopefully for publication, and wrote a blazing article which I sent to the Editor of the *Evening News*. I chose the *Evening News* as this was the newspaper that had published a picture of me on its front page. This showed me being bowled at in the nets of my brother's cricket school by members of the England cricket team who were about to tour Australia for the forthcoming Tests. The gist of the article was that we ladies should be armed so that while the men were away fighting we could defend the homeland. 'We already had a group six strong,' I said. 'Arm us and form similar detachments throughout the land,' I pleaded. The editor replied very courteously and said that he could not publish the article, for although he applauded our patriotism he did not think that his readers would approve of ladies going about killing people. His reply brought me up short. Infused as I was with all this white-hot patriotism I had never actually visualized shooting anyone *dead* — even a Nazi, although it was obvious that we were not about to be invaded by a horde of target-cards. That I was not the type to go killing anything living was soon to be proved.

Among other activities to help with the war effort I had become a part-time land girl. This resulted in my becoming very friendly with a handsome young farmer and, what was more, *he knew Cary Grant*. He was also a keen croquet player. He, I and four other young farmers used to repair to the local hostelry and spent many a pleasant summer evening playing croquet. Sometimes Babs came to stay with me for the weekend and she joined us in the croquet playing. We played darts as well and Babs showed that she could be a marksman too, for once, when it was her turn to play, she turned round on the bar stool on which she was sitting, and without getting up, nonchantly threw her dart from there, to hit double-top, to go right out and win the game for her side.

One weekend my farmer friend invited us both to a shoot. There were ten men as beaters, and it was all very exciting until someone emerged triumphantly from the wood with a dead hare slung over his arm. Its head was lolling sideways and blood poured on to the ground. I not only retired immediately from the shoot. I gave up my farmer, eating meat, my digs, and took up residence forthwith in a vegetarian guest-house. In any case I had decided that milking cows at 5 a.m. and threading one's way through cowpats was surely no way of fulfilling one's destiny.

The other guests at the vegetarian establishment were interesting to say the least. One was a Russian Jew, another a lady pacifist who showed me how to make and play a recorder, and for some incomprehensible reason, how to drop dead in seven different ways — one hoped that it was for histrionic purposes and not in anticipation of the expected invasion. I now

composed music and played it on the recorder for the delectation
of my fellow-guests. One of these was a girl of slant eyes and
ethnic orgins. She claimed that she came from Yugoslavia, but
it transpired that she originated from Bethnal Green. She had a
hang-up that she was a reincarnation of an Indian princess, and
she spent much of her time clad in a sari, performing Indian
dances for us, with much swaying and wafting of chiffon
scarves. I had shared my former digs with two young research
chemists. We became bosom pals, cycled the countryside and as
a trio had great times together. One was Philip from Somerset,
the other Sundra, a Buddhist and a Hindu of high caste, who
was writing a book on comparative religions of the world. He
decided to join me at the vegetarian guest-house. Although we
still remained a threesome Philip stayed in the digs as he
preferred a carnivorous habitat.

Sundra invited me to visit some friends of his who had a flat in
London, and many an interesting evening was spent with
compatriots of his from their far continent. Sometimes we took
along our friend of the sari so that she could live out her
reincarnation. As I was the only English member of the
company and was not knowingly a reincarnation of anybody, I
was the odd one, but I enjoyed the companionship of my new set
of friends, their cultured conversation and their many-flavoured
foods.

Another resident of the guest-house was a middle-aged
Hungarian of imposing stature and obvious erudition. The
books she had written, she said, had forewords by Freud
himself, for she was a psychologist. When she found out that I
worked at ICI she made a play at me. In the long and immensely
interesting conversations we had, she slipped in the odd leading
question. 'Where', she once asked me, almost as an aside 'do ICI
store their explosives?' Her eyes pierced mine hypnotically.
Without any hesitation and zombie-like, as though the words
were being dragged out of me, I answered; 'THEY ARE ALL
BURIED UNDER THE TURNIP FIELD ON OUR
FACTORY SITE HERE.' Of course it was a complete
fabrication. Our explosives' factories were all up north, which

was common knowledge, and of course I had no idea if or where the explosives were stored. We had tunnels under the turnip fields on the factory site but they were air-raid shelters, and where we slept when on fire duty. I rushed off to warn the powers-that-be before she had time to signal to the Luftwaffe to blow our sleeping quarters and us with them to smithereens, if indeed she were a Fifth Columnist. Apparently the authorities had their suspicions also and not very long after this our psychologist was interned for the duration. As she was escorted away, she turned to me with her compelling eyes full of reproach. 'I am very disappointed in you,' she said. 'You have let me down.' I felt most uncomfortable.

I made other unusual contacts through my fellow-guests. One day I found myself high up in a flat in Tottenham Court Road, in almost pitch darkness because of the black-out and almost curtainless windows, learning how to make Molotov Cocktails — home-made bombs — and how to put sugar in enemy petrol tanks when the invasion came. Babs was a bit worried about this assignation and took me there by car the first time, so that she could inform the police if I were spirited away without trace, to have ICI's secrets ferreted out of me. The fact that I worked in Treasurer's Department where salaries, cash payments and monthly statements were the order of the day and details of which, if divulged to the enemy, could have little effect on the course of the war, was beside the point. But all the others there appeared to be patriots from various parts of north-west London. I did, however, over a Molotov Cocktail, become friendly with a lady who was closely connected with the Free French. So henceforth I spent spirited evenings with the Free French at their particular rendezvous in Soho. Afterwards I would stay the night with my new friend at her flat, joined rather mysteriously by her son, a Ph.D., for he never showed up if the Free French were around and disappeared if ever they were.

Once, after a merry evening with the Free French at their Soho pub, she persuaded me to speak to a gathering of ladies at a Kensington hotel. I cannot remember the details, for having agreed when in a carefree mood, I needed some fortifying when it came to keeping my promise. She was determined to get me there for she had some 300 ladies awaiting my words of wisdom. Why I was qualified to speak or on what subject I cannot recall, if indeed I ever knew. However, I do remember being asked in question time: 'Is it true what the Nazis are supposed to be doing to the French women over there?' I replied in ringing tones, with a great deal of emotion and emphasis — for I had learned that trick of oratory from politicians' speeches — that 'I was sure that our boys would take care of *that*.' This drew vigorous rounds of applause and cheers. The meeting was declared a great success and my friend plied me with more drinks to recover.

I also found myself one evening in the flat of another patriot from the Molotov Cocktail set. This time I was entertained by a gentleman who was so much like a caricature of a Colonel in the British Army, but who, significantly was not serving, that he must surely be a fifth columnist, I thought, or at least a phoney. He kept persuading me to stay on, as his son, he said, was most anxious to meet me and was due home any moment. I wondered *why* his son should be so anxious to meet me, especially as so far he had not seemed keen to turn up. In spite of constant cajoling to stay I insisted that I must catch my last train, and eventually managed to leave with a certain amount of relief, because nobody knew where I was *that* time. The whole evening had seemed highly suspicious so I took no chances and reported the incident to the police. There was no opportunity of following up this bit of detection, as the glamour lady of the film weekly would have done, for the bombs started to rain down on London and visits there became more hazardous and less frequent.

No long after this the vegetarian guest-house closed down — ostensibly for lack of food, which had been delicious. ICI had taken over Digswell Park Conference House in old Welwyn to accommodate some of its Head Office employees and, when we were evacuated, I had opted out of living there as I did not relish the idea of communal life, but now, finding no other digs that appealed, I decided that I would give it a try.

I therefore indicated to Miss Buist, the Lady Supervisor of Head Office who lived there, that I would be pleased to join them at Digswell if anywhere could be made available for me to set up my dark-room. Relieved, no doubt, to get all her charges into the fold, she overlooked the effrontery of this request, and placed at my disposal the whole of the East Wing which was considered too damp for sleeping quarters. As photography interested many of the young men, they now came to help me. This led to a lot of unfounded gossip about the 'goings on' in the East Wing, but happily this stigma on my character was removed as the young men were called up.

Members of our sex could not be called up as ours was designated a reserved occupation, for we now took over the men's jobs and our work became much more responsible. However, some of us felt that we were not contributing enough to the war effort. True I had the Amazons at the ready should the need arise, but nobody wanted us so far. I was captain of a Fire Squad. This entailed being in charge of a small mobile fire engine and sleeping in the tunnel under the turnip field when on night duty; practising the fireman's lift, directing members of staff to crawl under tarpaulins of smoke — a most satisfactory operation when the victims were the bosses — and being trained by the Fire Chief in climbing up steep ladders and over the roofs at Digswell. When on night duty at the factory I used to load up my truck ready for any eventuality; photographic equipment and lamps to set up a studio for portraiture and still life while waiting for incendiary bombs to drop; books, boiler suit and tin helmet; food and the two half pints of beer allocated, whatever one's sex and — just in case — my .22 rifle. Sometimes, when we were in our bunks under the turnip field, I would blow the whistle for an emergency practice. We would then run out the fire engine, climb the fire escape, hose over shoulder, to the top of the factory roof and start the pump to put out non-existent fires. No incendiary bombs came our way, however, and we felt particulary ineffectual, for we could see the red glare in the sky, twenty-five miles away, as London burned. Sick with frustration, two of us went up to London to try to enrol in the

Auxiliary Fire Service, but we were turned down: they did not think that it was a good idea for us to travel fifty miles each day, nor was it feasible as it was uncertain that we should reach our destination. In any case, they added, we were needed where we were.

Some of us were doing part-time Land Army work, but hoeing miles and miles of mangel-wurzels did not seem dramatic enough when lives were being lost. We were allowed to join the Home Guard, referred to now as 'Dad's Army', but as auxiliaries only, to do the cooking and generally help behind the scenes. Our Unit, which consisted of men whose jobs were reserved and those awaiting call-up, was in charge of a section of the Great North Road. Here in a strategic position high above the road we awaited the Nazi hordes to come rumbling along in their tanks, so that we could hurl them back across the Channel. Although there were only some half a dozen rifles distributed among the men, the enormity of the task did not seem to daunt anyone and optimism ran high. I had the satisfaction of building a field kitchen — 'just like Churchill' I thought proudly, as I smacked cement and bricks together — and I had the added pleasure of doing some cooking.

As the imminent danger of invasion receded some of us wanted to take a more active part in winning the war and constantly lobbied the powers-that-be to be allowed to join the Women's Services. Meantime, in addition to these spare time contributions to the war effort, communal life lent itself to many recreational activities. We had musical evenings, organised parties and snowball fights in winter, attended WEA classes and went on cycling expeditions and long walks in the surrounding countryside. When I had practised at my brother's cricket school before the war, Jean Much had often accompanied me. She and I now arranged ladies' cricket matches and tried to put our expert coaching into practice. Peter, a friend who was awaiting call-up, and I managed to get up to the Lake District for some climbing and were able to visit London frequently for concerts. Once when we were at the Albert Hall, Myra Hess was the soloist and little did I know that one day I should come to live where once she had practised, for where I write adjoins the one-time barn which became a music room. She may even have slept in this very room, for Jetty Cottage was once used as an annexe for sleeping house guests, as it sometimes is now. Peter and I once organized a memorable skiing expedition by moonlight on the slopes of a cabbage field adjoining Digswell. An Austrian refugee, a Digswellian room neighbour, lent me her skis with the dire warning that skiing on two inches of snow in a cabbage field was a highly dangerous thing to attempt and could prove fatal. Certainly there were many falls, but luckily there was more laughter than groans.

Now that the Great North Road had not become congested with the Nazi hordes another friend and I used it for lorry-hops. We would, on occasion, book seats at the theatre at Stratford-on-Avon for the Saturday night performance, take up our stance in the morning on the Great North Road and arrive just in time for curtain up. Once after the performance and before travelling around the countryside the next day, Cecilia and I stayed the night in the first class compartment of a train in a siding, having been conducted there by a porter, who in the morning kindly brought us cups of tea.

These lorry-hopping expeditions became quite a feature when we had a spare Saturday and Sunday. We had several inviolate rules: we would only travel by lorry — private cars were allowed only in exceptional circumstances; trains were absolutely forbidden and we would take with us just 10s. apiece to supplement our picnic fare and for use in emergencies. I remember only breaking these rules twice; once finding ourselves in Somerset at dawn we allowed a BBC car to pick us up on its way to Bristol, our destination, as its speed would get us there more quickly and we had a crowded itinerary for the rest of Sunday. The second time was when we decided to visit my parents, who had evacuated themselves to join my sister-in-law and children in Aberdare in South Wales, after all the windows in our house in Surrey had been blasted out. We made good going on the Saturday and actually arrived in the valley below our destination just before dusk. As we wanted to reach

Aberdare by nightfall we decided to take a bus. It was full of workers and shoppers returning home and although it was only a short ride it was an experience I shall never forget. A red sun was setting over the misty Welsh mountains and flooded the bus with a ruby red light; the whole busload of passengers suddenly burst into song and sang as only the Welsh can, as we climbed the valley into the westering sun. We arrived in Aberdare by twilight, and intoxicated by the heady delights of our musical ride, we descended on my unsuspecting and astonished parents.

The next morning we travelled high over the Brecon Beacons and were finally deposited at a milk depot somewhere in Buckinghamshire shortly after midnight. Here we were given the choice of the 1 a.m. or 3 a.m. London-bound milk-tanker. We chose the 3 a.m. run so that we could be shown over the depot — a fortunate choice, for not only did we have a most interesting tour but we were regaled with glasses of milk and cream. We arrived at Digswell at 8 a.m. just in time for a bath and the second sitting at breakfast, before walking across the fields for our day's work and a short sleep before the evening's activities.

During the waits for the lorries of our choice I read for the first time *War and Peace* and was so enthralled with it that it became my No. 1 in the literary charts and I read it again in more comfortable circumstances. Some of our lorry drivers became our regulars and looked out for us. They all warned us of the dire perils of our mode of transport. Nevertheless, without exception, we found them to be true 'knights of the road'. In any case it was all just an adventure to us. To keep my hand in at writing I wrote up accounts of all these expeditions at great length and Cecilia, who was a secretary, typed them. They are apparently lost to posterity, for Cecilia who, with Jean, came to visit us last year, said that she no longer had them in her possession. So these epic tales are 'Missing presumed lost'.

She and I also took up tomato growing. We had two packet of seeds and experimented by growing them under different conditions: in the unheated conservatory at Digswell, in rich soil in the walled garden of the grounds there, on virgin soil near the turnip field on the factory site and, lastly, in a flower border beside our offices in the wooden huts. Two fertilizers were used: dried blood and cow manure and, as a control, we had a 'no fertilizer' group. I kept a progress chart showing the number of trusses per plant, the number and weight of fruit on each truss, and so on, to show the yield from the two different packets of seeds. Surplus fruit was bottled, for, by kind permission of the chief cook, we were allowed the use of the enormous kitchens at Digswell when she was off duty. As the permutations were numerous to say the least, this chart became about two yards long and was kept meticulously. In spite of its size, at the crucial moment at the end of the season I lost it, so our findings were never published. However I do remember that the virgin soil produced the biggest tomatoes but the skins were tough; the walled garden produced lush plants that grew like lofty trees and bore numerous fruit the size of marbles, and the cowpats as a fertilizer were a runaway success. The office border plants were the envy of all the men and we were persuaded to sell them at 6d. each, which was the going rate at the time, as they were considered superior to the commercially grown ones.

This gave us the idea that we would put the money aside for a trip round the world when the war was over. I added my mangel-wurzeling wages, which had recently been increased from 1s. 4d. per hour to the top rate of 1s. 8d. All this amassed to the satisfying sum, for those days, of £11 6s. 7d. which I put into National Savings Certificates for the duration. By that time Cecilia had moved to the US with her husband, and I was far too involved in this country to spare the time for a world trip. My savings, which had accumulated to a nice sum, went towards buying one of the earlier TV sets so that dad could watch the first Olympics Games to be televised, so enabling him to re-live his active and adventurous younger days when he sailed the Seven Seas, rounding Cape Horn under sail on passage to Valparaiso. By now at the age of seventy-five he was confined to a wheelchair having had both his legs amputated.

The tomato growing became an abiding interest. Here on the island they have become one of our main crops. Local folk come here especially to buy plants and the fruit, for they find the flavour delicious. With the long season and the wonderfully mild climate one can experiment endlessly to produce bumper crops, and I have the charts to prove it!

Literary efforts now turned to yet another magazine. A friend, Jane Lygo and I, together with Bill Bristowe, the Head of Central Staff Department, all three residents of Digswell, brought out a *Digswell Magazine*. This was considered a great success, especially by the three of us, and it became a regular feature of life there, and some of us have copies we have kept as a memento of those times we shared together.

Then at last came my big chance to fulfil my life's ambition. An advertisement appeared in the press for the job of sub-editor on *Woman's Journal*. Excited beyond measure I was called for an interview. This was conducted by the Managing Editor and the lady Editor. I explained that I was in fact in a reserved occupation, but I thought that I could arrange to get myself unreserved. While we were discussing this the Picture Editor came in and said that if they did not want me on the editorial side she would have me in the Photographic Department. Their depletion of staff due to call-up was giving me the chance of a lifetime. It was left that I should sort out the reserved occupation position.

Head in the clouds, I raced back to Digswell and almost hurled myself at Miss Buist, the Supervisor. She was a very kindly Scottish lady who was always most helpful to her 'girls', making us all feel like a family. Yes, she would do her best to get me released, for she knew of my ambitions. She was also a very clever lady. She pointed out that I ran the risk of being one of the first to go when their own staff returned at the end of the war, and somehow or other she implied, without actually putting it into words, that I should be deserting ICI in their hour of need. She would do her very best for me, but I was to think about it and let her know. Of course I felt I would be an absolute heel to leave and decided I must remain loyal to ICI.

In the course of time, after continued lobbying, those who wished were allowed to join the Women's Services and we were actually paid a retainer so that our jobs would be secure when we returned after the war. A farewell party was thrown for Cecilia, Jean and me, and paper sailor hats were made for each of us. We all three were joining the WRNS on the same day, but were destined not to meet together again until the summer of 1983 here on the island, forty years later.

My career in the WRNS, although full of exciting incidents, as could only be expected of one so incident prone, is not strictly part of 'The Author's Tale' for I did no writing at all.

An impressive looking Naval Officer, dripping with gold braid, addressed our gathering of newly recruited Wrens. He told us we were not, absolutely *not*, to keep a diary, in case it should fall into enemy hands. So I did not. By the same token I reckoned that I should not write letters either; so none were written except for guarded ones home. This gave rise to an item in the *Digswell Magazine* that Admiral 'Attie' had been sunk without trace, and to recriminations from all my friends that I had not answered a single letter throughout the war. In any case I had had a very busy war. Ever willing to help the Allied Cause I became very friendly with a contingent of Norwegian Naval Officers in Scotland and, but for my fortuitous posting *en route* for a commission at Greenwich Naval College, might have found myself spending the rest of my life in 'civvy street' in Norway.

After the war, responsibilities at home and ICI grew enormously, and with new interests and friends life became very crowded indeed. It became even more so when Di Sorby, she of the abortive treasure-hunting expedition to the island flagstaff, took a hand in my photographic career. Di, who had been a member of the Fire Brigade at Welwyn, and a leading light in the ICI Players, was a member of Publicity Department and took a great interest in my photography. My camera accompanied me, as usual, on all activities and post-war wanderings at home and abroad. Hours spent in the dark-room at the *Camera Club* in London and in my blacked-out bedroom at home produced exhibition prints, and Di showed some of my collection to the Art Editor. As a result he published many of these on the front and back covers of the ICI Magazine for which I was handsomely paid. He then commissioned me to take photographs on a regular basis and I became official photographer of the *Head Office News*, covering all kinds of subjects: Sporting events, amateur theatricals at the Fortune Theatre, office parties, presentations, bell-ringing in Southwark Cathedral, portraits of Heads of Departments and architecture to name a few. Others now commissioned me to take photographs, including portraits of people, babies, animals, weddings at Caxton Hall and elsewhere and receptions in Soho and fashionable hotels. With the fees that continued to be paid for the cover pictures photography was proving most lucrative. All these earnings were, of course, subject to income tax and I found making the returns complicated and a bit beyond me. Here it must be said that I found the Tax Officials most helpful. I would go along to the Tax Office with my scrappy bits of paper showing expenses; the Tax Officer would then work them all out for me and actually fill in the form. I was most surprised and gratified, especially as I was given advice that would benefit me and save me tax.

Now I was so busy with deadlines and dark-room work as well as working overtime in my Staff Department post that I scarcely had time to sleep, certainly not to write. Di, however, did write although not in a professional capacity. She inaugurated a Past and Present Club for lady members of ICI Head Office which is still flourishing. Now retired, in spite of ill-health, each year she writes a Newsletter, which entails much research and editing of her enormous correspondence, so that up-to-date news can be circulated to all members, some of whom are in hospital or housebound. Having launched me into professional photography Di now keeps everyone informed, in her Newsletters, of all our island activities and of my progress in authorship.

How then, after a lifetime of abortive attempts, did I at last come to write a book, and am even now finishing a second? I can take no credit for this myself.

When we first came to the island, after my early retirement, it was my dream that, in the sequestered calm of this splendid solitude I would at last be able to fulfil my childhood ambition of becoming an author; here, where there would be no people to distract me nor any pursuits to tempt me to dilly-dally along enticing side-tracks. That this dream was shattered is obvious from the foregoing *Tales*. Who or what was the catalysis? It was Babs!

Babs, who had started off as a toddler applauding my plays, and who seemingly graduated in no time at all to helping or guarding me at crucial moments in my life, now became directly responsible. Many books have been dedicated: 'To . . . without whose help and encouragement this book would never have been written.' I can and do so dedicate this book most wholeheartedly to Babs, but it would be more accurate to add that but for her it would have never been started.

A few years after we came to the island, Babs, in the course of her duties at school, was speaking to Terence Hanson, the rep. from Harrap, the publishers, about the educational books they were supplying to the school. The fact cropped up that she lived on an island. Terence Hanson pricked up his ears. 'Tell me more,' he said. Babs tossed him a few details about how we came to own an island in the first place. Intrigued, he said 'That sounds like the making of a book. Do you mind if I discuss it with Harrap staff in London?' 'Not at all', said Babs politely, little knowing that that innocuous phrase would light the fuse to a time bomb.

Shortly after this she received a letter from Paull Harrap, the Managing Director of Harrap, the gist of which was that they were interested in a book, and said that he would like to send his Senior Initiating Editor, Frank Waters, to discuss the matter.

Subsequently Frank Waters and his wife Denise came down to Looe with the intention of coming over here to the island with Babs to discuss the matter with us both. Somewhat to my relief, for by now I was quaking in my shoes — or rather gumboots — it was a wild wet day, with a forecast of worse to come. There was no possibility of getting over to the island, so Frank Waters took Babs to dinner at the Portbyhan Hotel, where she regaled him with tales of some of our adventures. He said that definitely they would like a book. After some general discussion Babs pin-pointed a major problem. 'How do *two* people write a book,' she asked, 'especially as I am on the mainland and my sister is on the island?' 'You have a point there,' said Frank Waters. 'Leave it with me.' Not long after his return to London he telephoned Babs. 'It has been decided', he said, 'that as your sister is living on the island all the time, she should write the book.'

Babs called me on the radio telephone. 'You are writing a book!' she said. Just like that.

I will not say that the idea did not appal me — it did. The sheer enormity of the task overwhelmed me. I was already like a demented being running the island — single-handed most of the time; coping with daffodils, cultivating the land, tending two greenhouses, printing, typing and doing the daily accounts, baking for day visitors and meeting them, coping with the cottagers, feeding the students, and attending to the generator and water-pump, as well as incidentals like feeding five pets, the goat and hens as well as myself, and trying to keep my hand in at pottery and assorted crafts — as a kind of relaxation. I felt, however, when I had recovered from the initial shock, that Fate had once again got me in its grasp. Just as it had brought us to the island, so now its finger pointed inexorably towards authorship. Was it not perhaps written in the stars? How else should I have known at the age of six that one day I would become an author, albeit a lifetime away. Or is it perhaps that if one wishes hard enough and long enough, the wish will one day be granted? Paull Harrap and Frank Waters gave me the initial stimulus for the first book. Now Simon Scott, the present Editorial Director of Harrap, has entered the field and his very real encouragement has helped me when I have faltered on the way to finishing this sequel.

Little did I know when Babs announced 'You are writing a book!' that I would be writing two books; that I would have enough material for a third, a fourth or even a fifth. But would I have the time?

What a pity that I did not start at the age of six.